There was once a widower who had two bright, young daughters who were so curious about everything that they kept asking questions. Questions, questions, questions. And though their father was able to answer some of their questions, there were many that he just couldn't answer. And he began to feel that they needed someone who could. So he decided to send them to live with the wise old man who lived on the hill. Which was what you did in those days.

So off went the two girls to live with the wise old man who lived on the hill. And they continued to ask questions. Questions, questions, questions. But unlike their father, the wise old man always had an answer. He could answer every single question they asked.

At first, this was delightful. But as time went by, the girls began to find it a little irritating that, no matter what they asked, the old man always had an answer. And as time went by some more, they began to find it very irritating. So they began to search for ways to catch him out.

One day, one sister ran up to the other with a beautiful, bright blue butterfly in her hands. 'I've got this great idea,' she said. 'I've just found this butterfly, and I thought I'd hide it in my hands and go and ask the old man whether it's alive or dead. If he says it's dead, I'll open my hands and let it fly out. If he says it's alive, I'll give a quick, hard squeeze and open my hands and say "Wrong, it's dead!" So whatever he says, he can't win.' 'Brilliant!' said her sister, and off they went to find the wise old man.

Eventually they found him, sitting on a rock under a eucalyptus tree. The girls rushed up. 'Oh wise old man,' said the sister with the butterfly, 'I've got this butterfly in my hands, and I want you to tell me if it's alive or dead.'

The wise old man looked at the two sisters for a moment and thought. Then he smiled. 'My dears,' he said, 'the butterfly is …'

In Your Hands

NLP in ELT

Jane Revell and Susan Norman

Saffire PRESS

Copyright © 1997 Jane Revell and Susan Norman

Jane Revell and Susan Norman assert their moral and legal right
to be identified as the authors of this book.

First published September 1997
Reprinted May 1998, May 1999, November 2000

Published by

Saffire Press
37 Park Hall Road
East Finchley
London, England
N2 9PT

Fax: +44 (0)20 8444 0339
Email: hugh@saffirepress.co.uk

The authors and publisher welcome comments on this or their other publications.

Printed in Great Britain

ISBN 1 901564 00 2

THIS BOOK WAS BORN OUT OF FIRE …

The authors first met in front of the notice boards as they were deciding which sessions to sign up for at the SEAL Conference in 1991. Susan was keen to do the firewalk. Jane didn't really like the sound of walking barefoot across burning coals. She was scared. But she liked the look of Susan. So they did the firewalk together. Looking up all the time. And looking forward.

Since then they've hardly looked back.

CONTENTS

❦   Audio recording available

Acknowledgements

We would both like to thank

- Anne Murray-Robertson for all her help and advice right from the very beginnings of the project and without whom we might have fallen into many pits

- Our readers: Eleanor May-Brenneker, Marisa Carrara, John Eaton, Izabella Hearn, Gisela Langé, Janet Olearski, Katrina Patterson, Philip Prowse and Dominique Vouillemin, for their helpful and encouraging comments, and Isobel Fletcher de Téllez for her pains-taking editorial work

- Mario Rinvolucri for his enthusiasm and support for the project, and for his warm and generous comments on the back cover

- Julia Vinton, who not only designed the cover and the layout of the book, but held our hands throughout the novelty and excitement of putting it together on screen. And Rosine Faucompré, our project manager, who led us through the printing jungle without a single scratch

- The people whose ideas we've borrowed: for versions of some of the stories – Christina Hall (The Monster and the Watermelon), Alix Nadelman (The Wise Woman and the Hats) and Nick Owen (The Wise Teacher and the Jar); for 'relaxes' instead of 'tenses' – Gerry Schmidt

- Mal Peet on the visual side for his wonderful and witty drawings

- Hugh Kermode on the auditory side for his musical creations, for his skilful recording and editing of the stories and for making it fun

- Andy Cowle of Keltic and Nick Ridley of English Teaching Professional for their splendid advice and support

- And, last but certainly not least, Hugh L'Estrange, for putting the book together and doing all the non-glorious stuff behind the scenes, and for just being there

Jane would like to thank

- Susan Norman, for suggesting that we write the book in the first place, and for being such a brilliant co-author

- My mother, who thwarted my ambition to go to secretarial college at the age of 18 by telling me, 'Don't waste your time writing down other people's ideas when you've got so many of your own!'

- Janet Olearski, for suggesting I go to the 1991 SEAL Conference, which was the beginning of a lot of new things in my life

- Those NLP teachers who taught me by *being* what they were teaching, and in particular, the two Judiths: Judith DeLozier and Judith Lowe, with their dynamic yet down-to-earth approach

- All the teachers I have ever trained or worked with, who have shared their ideas or who have given me really useful feedback

- Storytellers and writers of stories, past and present, for inspiring and entertaining me as a child, and for providing me with rich source material as a storyteller myself, as mother, teacher, trainer and therapist

◆ Max and Tamzyn L'Estrange, for putting up with neglect, clothes stuck for days in the wash and frequent take-away meals, while the book got written

Susan would like to thank

◆ All those who taught and inspired my EFL teaching, in particular Nick McIver; John Haycraft and others at International House; Mario Rinvolucri; Vera Birkenbihl, Paul Smith, Jeremy Smith, John Kent, Sue Swift and others from 'Trento'; and the students, especially the 'AYE family'

◆ My teachers and helpers in yoga, meditation and visualisation: Charles Lovell, Lena Waters, Terri Tree, Barry Tomalin, Penny Brohn (albeit unwittingly)

◆ The supporters of my early writing, especially Michael Cass and Peter Murphy

◆ My NLP teachers, especially Richard Bandler, Paul McKenna, Michael Breen and Jane Revell

◆ John Norman, my husband, for the intellectual challenges, the drama techniques and for supportively holding the fort so that I could write

◆ Brian de la Plain, my father, thanks to whom it was many years before I realised there was any alternative to positive thinking

◆ Jane Revell for the generous co-operation, the new perspectives and the swimming

Thanks too to all the other people we haven't mentioned who have also contributed significantly to this book and to our development.

We won't hold any of you responsible.

The authors and publisher would like to thank the following for permission to reproduce copyright material:

◆ Health Communications Inc. for *'Follow your dreams'* (page 59) from *Chicken Soup for the Soul,* ©Jack Canfield, Mark Victor Hansen

◆ AVANTA, The Virginia Satir Network (2104 SW 152nd Street, Suite 2, Burien, WA 98166) for *'The Five Freedoms'* (page 67) from *Making Contact.* All rights reserved

◆ Marianne WILLIAMSON, *A Return to Love* (page 137)[HarperCollins Publisher] 1992

Attempts have been made to obtain permission to use other quotations.

◆ Robert B DILTS *Effective Presentation Skills* (page 80) [Meta Publications] 1994

◆ Mary Catherine BATESON *Composing a Life* (page 62) [The Atlantic Monthly Press] 1989

◆ Paulo COELHO *The Pilgrimage* (page 62) [HarperCollins Publishers] 1992

◆ Marcel PROUST *In Search of Lost Time* (page 83) [Vintage] 1996

We also wish to express our special appreciation to Zedcor, Inc., Tucson, Arizona for permission to use so many of their delightful DeskGallery and ArtToday images throughout the book.

If any other copyright holders have been inadvertently overlooked, the publisher will be pleased to make the necessary arrangements at the first opportunity.

Until one is committed,
there is hesitancy,
the chance to draw back,
always ineffectiveness.

Concerning all acts of initiative
(and creation),
there is one elementary truth,
the ignorance of which
kills countless ideas
and splendid plans –
that the moment
one definitely commits oneself,
then Providence moves too.

All sorts of things occur to help one
that would never otherwise have occurred.

Whatever you can do
or dream you can, begin it.

Boldness has genius,
power and magic in it.

BEGIN IT NOW!

GOETHE

Introduction

This book is for everyone who has heard of NLP but isn't exactly sure what it is. It's a book for teachers interested in their own personal development and that of the learners for whom they are responsible. It is for people who want to become better teachers and want to help their students become better learners. And it is for anyone who wants to live life more fully.

Our aim is to give you a real sense of what NLP is all about, in a short-winded and readable way. We also aim to inspire you with what we say and with the thought-provoking quotations and asides we have inserted throughout. We draw implications for teaching and learning, and provide a variety of activities so you can experience the benefits of NLP both in your personal life and in your teaching.

NLP is like a complex 3-D structure, but a book is linear and we have chosen to present the information in an order which we hope will make it accessible and help your understanding grow. However, all the ideas are interrelated, and those at the end of the book are just as relevant as those at the beginning and in the middle.

We suggest that you read to the end of this book to get an overview of the subject so that you know where any particular activity fits into the whole. We also suggest that you try the activities out on yourself before using them with anyone else. In the 'Transfer to Teaching' sections we suggest ways of using the activities with students, both to help them become better learners, and to improve their English. We also recommend that you share the information about NLP with your students.

We assume that you are already a competent teacher and that you have strategies for presenting information, pre-teaching items, getting your students involved, organising groupwork, pairwork and class discussions, etc. We have given pointers rather than step by step 'recipes', in the hope that you will make the material your own and adapt it to the language level, needs and preferences of your students.

> Don't stop here. Take the ideas which work for you. Work with them, add to them and share them with others.

Our involvement with NLP has developed over a period of time. It began when we had already been teaching English as a Foreign Language and writing EFL materials for a number of years. It is inevitable that the line between 'pure' NLP and our interpretation of it has become blurred. A lot of the ideas seemed very familiar to us – as we hope they will to you. Many of them seemed to justify what we were doing already. Some gave an exciting new direction to our lives and our teaching.

At the same time we do have questions about some areas, which we discuss in the course of the book. Our approach is to keep an open mind, while we explore and experience further.

> *"You can never step into the same river twice."*
> **ZEN SAYING**

We believe in what we have written here, but that doesn't mean you have to! Please read the book with a healthy scepticism and match it against your own experience. Above all, enjoy it.

NLP is constantly growing and changing. We are constantly growing and learning and changing. You are too and we hope this book will help.

Although NLP terminology can be a bit daunting, we have decided to use it, mainly for ease of cross-referencing with other books. All NLP terms are explained in clear language within the text.

How this book is arranged

The main elements of NLP – the 'big chunks', if you like – are the **presuppositions,** and the **core concepts.** We have presented them alternately in an attempt to steer a course towards a fuller understanding of NLP and to aid the process of self-discovery and empowerment.

The four pillars – outcomes, rapport, sensory acuity and flexibility – are the cornerstones of the **core concepts**, but you will meet others, namely 'VAKOG', Submodalities, Anchoring, Metaprograms and Modelling.

Between the presuppositions and the core concepts there are various NLP **models** and **techniques,** such as Life levels, Timelines and Perceptual positions. Other models and techniques are incorporated within the larger sections.

Understanding the (sometimes unconscious) influence of **language** in our lives is vital to the knowledge and practice of NLP and will be of particular interest to language teachers. Special sections of the book examine the literal meaning of the language we use, as well as ways of using language to effect positive change. We also offer specific suggestions for using this approach in ELT.

All sections are clearly signalled both in the contents page and in the header at the top of each page.

NLP also incorporates **stories** and **guided fantasies** which act as metaphors and allow the non-conscious mind to work its magic. You'll find some of our favourites at intervals throughout the book. You are welcome to photocopy these pages and use them in the classroom. Items with this symbol [ᴈᴄ] in the contents page can be found on the accompanying cassette. Sit back and listen. Play them to your students. Enjoy them.

Caveat

NLP techniques can be extremely powerful. They are based on thought and behaviour patterns that successful people adopt most of the time and that most of us adopt some of the time. However, there is a big difference between reading about techniques and practising them. If you are interested in finding out more about NLP, we recommend that you follow a recognised course of instruction. If you want to try out some of the techniques, try them out on yourself first. If you experiment with other people, please make sure that it is with their knowledge and consent.

NLP has been accused of being manipulative. It is a tool. Like a knife. Like a knife it can be used for good or for bad. It is up to you how you use it. You can cut bread with it or you can threaten someone with it. The NLP practitioners we know are all busy slicing bread rather than people and are doing a tremendous amount of good.

NLP is designed to give people choices and help them to achieve their goals and their potential. The more we understand and use its techniques, the greater the opportunities for improving communication and achieving human excellence.

What is NLP?

Neuro-Linguistic Programming is an attitude to life. It is also a collection of techniques, patterns and strategies for assisting effective communication, personal growth and change, and learning. It is based on a series of underlying assumptions about how the mind works and how people act and interact.

The aim of NLP is to enhance the quality of people's lives by helping them to identify and achieve their outcomes, and to interact more effectively with others. It is a means of achieving intra-personal and inter-personal excellence.

The **neuro** part of NLP is concerned with how we experience the world through our five senses and represent it in our minds through our neurological processes.

The **linguistic** part of NLP is concerned with the way the language we use shapes, as well as reflects, our experience of the world. We use language – in thought as well as in speech – to represent the world to ourselves and to embody our beliefs about the world and about life. If we change the way we speak and think about things, we can change our behaviour. We can also use language to help other people who want to change.

The **programming** part of NLP is concerned with training ourselves to think, speak and act in new and positive ways, in order to release our potential and reach those heights of achievement which we previously only dreamt of. (Dreaming of them first certainly helps, as you will see.)

A brief history of NLP

In the early 1970s, an American professor of linguistics, John Grinder, and a psychology student, Richard Bandler, wanted to find 'the difference that makes the difference' between mere mortals and people who excel. They studied some amazingly successful therapists (chiefly Virginia Satir, Fritz Perls and Milton Erickson) and found that they all followed similar patterns in relating to their clients and in the language they used, and that they all held similar beliefs about themselves and about what they were doing. It was particularly interesting that these experts appeared to be unaware of the existence of these patterns and beliefs.

Bandler and Grinder decided to find out what the specific patterns and beliefs were and to see if they could be learnt by other people. Together with co-workers (Leslie Cameron-Bandler, Judith DeLozier and Robert Dilts, among others), they developed these patterns and beliefs into something they called 'Neuro-Linguistic Programming'.

NLP has relevance far beyond the field of psychotherapy where it originated. Its central ideas are now being incorporated into many approaches to communication, learning and change: personal development, management, sales and marketing and – significantly for us – education.

Bandler and Grinder certainly never intended to found a school of psychotherapy, and NLP does not pretend to be a scientific theory of behaviour. It is based on observation and experience. The criterion for inclusion is, 'Does it work?'

The NLP presuppositions

At the heart of NLP are the presuppositions, which guide the whole approach and which underlie the thoughts, interpretations and suggestions throughout this book. They do not need to be accepted as the absolute truth, but acting as if they were true can make a world of difference in your life and in your teaching.

Some of the presuppositions are not unique to NLP. Some of them are identical to or very similar to our own long-standing beliefs. Others were not already part of our (conscious) belief system, and we have become aware of them through NLP.

- Mind and body are interconnected: they are parts of the same system, and each affects the other
- The map is not the territory: we all have different maps of the world
- There is no failure, only feedback … and a renewed opportunity for success
- The map becomes the territory: what you believe to be true either is true or becomes true
- Knowing what you want helps you to get it
- The resources we need are within us
- Communication is non-verbal as well as verbal
- The non-conscious mind is benevolent
- Communication is non-conscious as well as conscious
- All behaviour has a positive intention
- The meaning of my communication is the response I get
- Modelling excellent behaviour leads to excellence
- In any system, the element with the greatest flexibility will have the most influence on that system

---

THINK

- How do you interpret each presupposition?
- What would things be like if the opposite of the presupposition were true?
- What are the implications of each presupposition for you
      a) personally?   b) as a teacher?
- What are the implications for your students as learners?
- Are there any presuppositions that you would want to question?

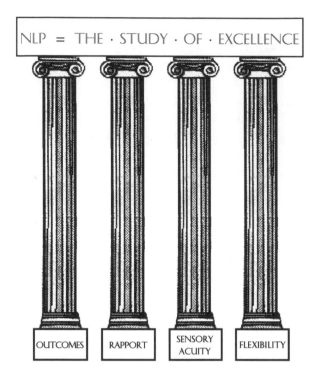

The four pillars of NLP

NLP rests on four pillars. These could be said to be the 'mind' of NLP: the fundamental concepts which support everything else.

OUTCOMES in NLP means something very similar to goals or objectives (rather than the everyday English meaning of 'results'). NLP is very much an 'achievement-oriented technology' and is based on the belief that knowing precisely what you want helps you to get it.

RAPPORT is the heart of successful communication with other people. It's a way of maximising similarities and minimising differences between people at a non-conscious level. Without it, communication can fail, conflict can arise and everyone tends to lose out. With it, communication is positive and harmonious, and everyone is more likely to be happy and to achieve their outcomes.

SENSORY ACUITY is to do with really noticing what another person is communicating – often non-consciously and often non-verbally. It is to do with observing carefully and not making quick assumptions or judgements, so that we can respond appropriately and with maximum rapport.

FLEXIBILITY means doing something different if what you're doing isn't working and isn't getting you what you want. And it's having the range of skills and techniques to do something else different if that doesn't work. And something else, and something else, and something else – until you get there.

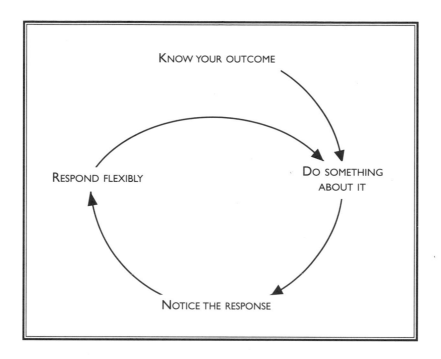

The Basic Action Model

Each step of this model relates to one of the four pillars. The first step, *know your outcome,* is to do with knowing very clearly what you want to achieve. The second step, *do something about it,* is almost bound to involve other people, hence the crucial importance of rapport. (Even if the action is solitary, rapport with yourself is essential.) The third step, *notice the response,* links with sensory acuity. And the fourth step, *respond flexibly,* is all to do with having a range of options about what to do next.

Although this model may in some ways seem obvious, it isn't always what we do. We're often not very clear about our outcomes, either in the personal or the professional sphere. Nor do we always act in accordance with what we want – especially if our outcomes are unclear in the first place. Sometimes we are not particularly flexible: if what we do doesn't work, we often tend to do the same thing again, to see if it will work this time. And sometimes we blame someone or something else for the fact that it didn't work the first time.

If you don't recognise yourself in any of this, you can put this book down immediately.

THINK

Start with the first step of the model:

What is your intended outcome in reading this book?

What do you want to achieve? Write it down.

Q

QUIZ – TEACHING AND LEARNING

Everything we do in the classroom is based on what we believe about teaching and learning. Our purpose in this section is not to tell you what to believe. Perish the thought! However, you might like to use this quiz to help you to think about what you believe and to know where we are coming from. So, do you agree with the following statements? Make some notes here before reading on.

1 The most important person in the classroom is the student.

❑ Agree ❑ ??? ❑ Disagree

2 The responsibility for learning lies with the teacher.

❑ Agree ❑ ??? ❑ Disagree

3 There is no one right way to teach or learn anything.

❑ Agree ❑ ??? ❑ Disagree

4 Learning is a serious business.

❑ Agree ❑ ??? ❑ Disagree

5 Mistakes are good.

❑ Agree ❑ ??? ❑ Disagree

6 The teacher's job is to teach the subject.

❑ Agree ❑ ??? ❑ Disagree

7 You should leave your private life outside the classroom.

❑ Agree ❑ ??? ❑ Disagree

8 It is essential to teach grammar to language learners.

❑ Agree ❑ ??? ❑ Disagree

9 'Chalk and talk' is still the most efficient way to teach.

❑ Agree ❑ ??? ❑ Disagree

10 The teacher should know all the answers.

❑ Agree ❑ ??? ❑ Disagree

TEACHING AND LEARNING – WHAT WE BELIEVE

1 The most important person in the classroom is the student.
Of course we agree. We believe in the importance of self-esteem and that each student has the right to be considered individually. Each student is important. All the students are important. And of course we disagree. The teacher is important too. We believe in respect and consideration for and from everyone in the classroom.

2 The responsibility for learning lies with the teacher.
Yes – and no. The only person who can learn is the learner. Learning is a shared responsibilityand depends on co-operation between students and teacher. We let the students know what we're doing and why, both for the immediate benefits in the classroom and to give them the ability to continue learning beyond the classroom. 'Learning to learn' is an essential component of our lessons.

3 There is no one right way to teach or learn anything.
Different students learn in different ways, just as they have different needs, different personalities, and different contributions to make. There may be one right way for each person to learn, but even so, most people benefit from variety. Many roads are good. We'll try anything that works. What is important is to find the right way for each individual and to be flexible in our approach.

4 Learning is a serious business.
Of course it is. And that's why it's crucially important to laugh about it, have fun and enjoy it. We believe that people learn best when they're enjoying themselves.

5 Mistakes are good.
Making a mistake when you're driving a car can cost someone's life! On the other hand, practice makes perfect, and there are bound to be mistakes while we're practising. The important thing is that our students know it's OK to make mistakes and so are happy to take risks and experiment while they are learning.

6 The teacher's job is to teach the subject.
Yes … but. The teacher's job is to teach the students in such a way as to help them to learn the subject. We are educators and while teaching language, we are also communicating our values and beliefs.

7 You should leave your private life outside the classroom.
Rhubarb! Use your humanity, your experience. Use theirs. Of course, the focus needs to be on those aspects of life that enhance language learning, but we acknowledge when we're feeling bad – and good – and encourage learners to do the same. We also encourage them to put their problems aside in the classroom and use the time for learning. For our part, teaching is a terrific way of letting go of our own worries.

8 It is essential to teach grammar to language learners.
It's essential to teach grammar, functions, vocabulary, the four language skills, pronunciation, fluency, accuracy … and lots more. We'll teach anything that helps students learn to use the language better. It's not 'either/or'. We believe in 'and/also'.

9 'Chalk and talk' is still the most efficient way to teach.
We disagree, although we do still occasionally do it, along with all the other ways. In the main, we believe in eliciting rather than telling. We believe in a multi-sensory approach and learning through activity. We believe in engaging the learner's intelligence and emotions.

10 The teacher should know all the answers.
Whoops! If that were true, the profession would disappear! However, we do feel that teachers should always be learning and that our main responsibility is to learn how to help other people learn more effectively. We know we don't know everything. Our students know it too. So we share what we do know and we share the quest of finding out what we don't know. Teaching is an excellent way of finding out exactly what we do know and of learning more – which is why we encourage our students to be the teacher sometimes too.

This book will not tell you all the answers. We're learning more even as we write it. However, just as it's helped us to formulate some of our own answers, we hope it will help you to find more of yours.

Mind and body are interconnected

Your mind affects your body and your body affects your mind. This presupposition is not unique to NLP. It is shared by many other bodies(!) of thought. If your state of mind is good, you tend to feel good physically too. And the better your body feels, the better your mind functions. It is also true that activating the body activates the mind. Educational Kinesiology (also known as Edu-K or Brain Gym) is a system in which physical activities are used to produce connections in the brain and to enhance learning. Conversely, Milton Erickson, the famous hypno-therapist and one of the original 'models' for NLP, found that rehearsing body movements in his mind enabled him to overcome much of the paralysis caused by polio.

THINK HOW IT WOULD BE IF MIND AND BODY WERE **NOT** CONNECTED...

A positive mental attitude can keep people healthy, while stress and tension can result in 'dis-ease'. The important thing is not what happens but how you react to what happens. You always have a choice about how you behave.

How are you feeling right now? Don't move. Keep quite still. Notice how your body is positioned. Don't move. Just notice. Which muscles are tense? How is your breathing – is it deep or shallow? What is the expression on your face? Are you frowning or smiling? Notice particularly any tension you are holding on to. How are you feeling emotionally? Positive or negative?

Now move your body into a more balanced position, take a deep breath in, relaxing your stomach as you do so, and as you breathe out, relax and let go of any tension. Smile. Feel better?

It is much easier to avoid stress and tension if you stop it building up. Get into the habit of checking the state of your body and mind. Look for the funny side of things. Laugh. Breathe deeply. Get plenty of fresh air. Do physical activity regularly and make time to relax. It doesn't need to take a lot of time. 'Little and often' is most effective.

And if you can't even find the few minutes, and you don't feel good, then fake it. Behave as you would if you felt good – and notice the difference.

Break state

If you or your students are upset about something, or just getting a bit bogged down, you can 'break state' by choosing consciously to do something else. Shake your hands, say a tongue twister, count backwards in threes from 100, stretch and yawn, do something physical – the one we specially like is 'gorilla thumps': bang your chest with both fists and say 'aaaahh' very loudly.

:: **Implications** ::

- Think yourself into a really good state for doing whatever it is you want or need to do, including teaching and learning.

- Do physical activities in the classroom to optimise the learning state of your learners. Controlled breathing, physical exercises and relaxation activities all relax and recharge learners to enable them to learn more effectively.

- Encourage smiling and laughter in the classroom. It keeps people healthy and helps them learn.

- Deal with problems and worries straight away. Encourage students to share any distracting problems if they want to, and/or use strategies to help them to leave them aside temporarily.

- School itself can be a great source of anxiety for many students. Students learn best from 'high challenge, low stress' activities.

～～～ MIND YOUR EMOTIONS ～～～

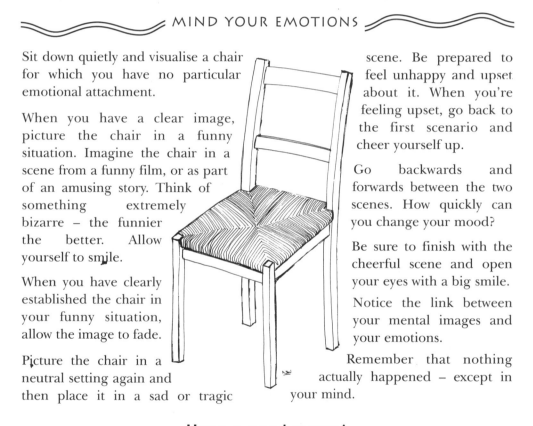

Sit down quietly and visualise a chair for which you have no particular emotional attachment.

When you have a clear image, picture the chair in a funny situation. Imagine the chair in a scene from a funny film, or as part of an amusing story. Think of something extremely bizarre – the funnier the better. Allow yourself to smile.

When you have clearly established the chair in your funny situation, allow the image to fade.

Picture the chair in a neutral setting again and then place it in a sad or tragic scene. Be prepared to feel unhappy and upset about it. When you're feeling upset, go back to the first scenario and cheer yourself up.

Go backwards and forwards between the two scenes. How quickly can you change your mood?

Be sure to finish with the cheerful scene and open your eyes with a big smile.

Notice the link between your mental images and your emotions.

Remember that nothing actually happened – except in your mind.

Have a good worry!

Set aside ten minutes to think about all the things you have worried about in the last 24 hours and all the things you might need to worry about in the next 24 hours.

Now worry about them. Do it properly. Don't stop before your ten minutes is up. If you find your mind drifting off to something nice, be strong and drag it back to the worries.

"If I spent as much time doing the things I worry about as I do worrying about them, I wouldn't have anything to worry about."

BERYL PFIZER

Make a date to do the same tomorrow – and let go of your worries until then. If you suddenly think of something you forgot to worry about, write it down so you can really do it justice at your next worry session! With practice you will be able to get your worrying down to five, or even two, minutes a day.

Stress busters

Make a note of things you do to relieve stress and aid relaxation. Ask other people for their stress busters too. Try them out. Some of ours are taking a warm bath, swimming, gardening, going for a walk, drawing, Jane works out in the gym, Susan does yoga and anything that restores a sense of perspective and turns mountains back into molehills.

 LIVE LONGER WITH THIS THREE-MINUTE EXERCISE

The following instructions are on the cassette, so you can just *relax and enjoy it.*

Sit in a balanced, upright position with both feet flat on the floor, hands resting on your thighs. Sit up straight and feel your head balanced on the top of your spine. If you feel comfortable doing so, close your eyes. Take a deep breath in, keeping your shoulders still and relaxing your tummy as you do so. Now breathe out, pulling your stomach in.

Next time you breathe out, you're going to relax your body from the top down. Breathe in again, and as you breathe out relax your face, relax your neck, relax your shoulders, relax your arms, relax your hands, your abdomen, your bottom, your legs, your feet. Finish breathing out. And let go. Let all the tension drain out through your feet into the ground.

Once again, consciously relax your body from the top down. Breathe in … and as you breathe out, relax your face, your neck, your shoulders, your arms, your hands, your abdomen, your bottom, your legs, your feet. Let go.

Think about the link between the words 'respiration', 'inspiration / to inspire' and 'to expire'.

One more time, and this time as you relax, say mentally to yourself (in English) 'I'm relaxing my face, I'm relaxing my neck, I'm relaxing my shoulders, …' and so on. So, breathe in … and in your own time, as you breathe out, relax.

And now, take another deep breath in, and smile. And breathe normally. And stretch. And open your eyes.

Sometimes, in order to relax a part of the body, it helps to tense it first. You *gently* bring just enough tension into your whole body in order to feel it – your face, torso, arms, legs, hands, feet, everywhere – and then let it go.

By 'relaxation' we mean a conscious letting go of stress and tension in body and mind. We don't mean slumping in front of the telly or going out for a meal. These may provide a change of pace from working, but they are really leisure activities which often leave you more tired than before. Genuine relaxation calms and energises at the same time.

 TRANSFER TO TEACHING

We also do this activity regularly with learners. It's a great way to counteract tiredness and boredom – or high spirits – and to get learners into a good learning state.
What language would you need to pre-teach before doing this activity with learners for the first time? Who could you use it with? Who couldn't you use it with? Do you think your learners would take to this type of activity readily? If you felt you would need to convince them of its value, how would you do it?

Guided fantasy: The deserted beach

Make sure you're sitting in an upright position with both feet flat on the floor, hands resting comfortably on your thighs. Take a deep breath, and relax.

Close your eyes for a moment, and imagine that you are walking alone along a deserted beach. You are very safe and will not be disturbed.

Make a clear picture in your mind's eye. Look around you as you walk. What can you see? Notice the colours. Look out to sea as far as the horizon. Is the sea calm? Is it rough? Are there any boats? Or birds? What kind of day is it? Sunny? Cloudy?

Hear the sound of the waves. Hear the sound of your footsteps in the sand or on the pebbles. What other sounds are you aware of? Can you hear seagulls?

Feel the air against your skin. Breathe it in. How does it smell? How does it taste? Feel the movement of your body as you walk. Feel the beach under your feet.

Go right up to the water's edge and put your hand into the water. How does that feel? Put your wet hand against your face. Is it cold? Can you smell the sea? Can you taste the salt?

You may feel like taking off your shoes and socks to have a paddle. Or you may feel like taking off the rest of your clothes to have a swim. Or you may feel like sitting for a while and gazing out to sea. Or you may feel like continuing your walk along the beach. Do whatever you feel like doing. You will have half a minute of real time which is all the time you need. And, whatever you do, be very aware of everything that you see and hear and feel. And be glad to have this chance to be alone in such a beautiful place …

And now prepare to leave, knowing you can revisit this place any time you choose. When you're ready, take a deep breath, and, with a sense of gladness, come back to the room.

MEET YOUR MIND

Think about the following questions about the guided fantasy, 'the deserted beach'.

🜄 Could you see a clear picture or a sort of fuzzy blur, or nothing at all, or what? If you couldn't see a picture as such, imagine what your picture *would* be like.

🜄 How is what you saw different from what you would see if you were on a beach?

🜄 Were you looking at yourself from the outside or were you inside? Can you do both? What are the main differences?

🜄 Did you hear any sounds (apart from the cassette)? What sounds? Did you hear a voice or voices? Were you speaking or was it someone else? Describe the sounds and voice(s).

🜄 Could you actually feel the beach beneath your feet? And the air? And the water? Could you smell and taste salt? How is your imagination different from reality?

By the way, everyone's mind works differently. Ask other people (your students?) to do the above task and then compare their answers with yours. Find out as many differences as possible.

Classroom audit

Walk into your classroom (or imagine yourself there). Look around. Note ten things you could do to make it more comfortable for your students. Is there adequate fresh air – or could you go outside occasionally? Can you move the furniture? Put pictures on the wall? Draw / write something welcoming on the board? What about curtains or fabrics? Flowers? Cushions? Lockable cupboards for keeping things in? Could you play music? Have fresh water available and encourage students to drink often. Enlist your students' help. Take turns to bring in sweets for a quick energy fix. Choose one thing to do immediately. Do it.

"Worry is misuse of the imagination."
MARY CROWLEY

Now, how about their mental comfort?

WORDSTORM

As you read through this list of words, think back over the key points of this section. Add any other words which help you remember what you want to remember.

mind • body • mind power • mental state • stress buster • release tension • physical activity • relax • live longer • 3-minute exercise • breathe • positive • negative • energy • respiration • inspiration • gladness • interconnections • exercise • worry • comfort • imagine • beach • fantasy • emotions

The Wise Woman and the Hats

nce upon a time a wise woman went to give a lecture in a faraway town. As she began to speak, she looked around the hall at the twenty or so people in her audience and she noticed something rather strange. They were all wearing hats. And very remarkable hats they were too.

The village gardener wore a hat that was absolutely covered in weeds. A young mother wore a sort of bonnet made out of babies' nappies. One man had a beret with tax forms pinned all over it. Another had a bowler hat with three telephones on it. Someone else had a fur hat which had almost disappeared under hundreds of unpaid bills. The farmer in the back row had a calf on her head. And the lady in the front row had a sort of Paddington Bear hat covered with chocolates. And there were many more remarkable hats.

The wise woman paused in what she was saying. 'I've been noticing what splendid hats you're all wearing,' she said. 'But I do think that you'll be able to hear what I'm saying a lot better, if you take them off. Why don't you put your hats at the back of the hall for the time being? You can pick them up again after the lecture.'

The people in the audience got up and went to the back of the hall. They took off their hats and put them down. The farmer laid her calf gently in the hat covered in weeds. Then they went back to their seats.

'Thank you,' said the wise woman. And she went on with her lecture. And she was right. The people in the audience could hear much better without their hats.

The map is not the territory

There is the world. And there is our experience of the world. They are not the same thing. A map of Italy represents Italy. It is not Italy itself. We all experience 'reality' in our own way. And though we tend to think that our way is the one and only right way, it is only one way, one map. And other people have other ways, other maps. The map is not the territory.

Used as a metaphor, this works at all sorts of levels. The obvious one is to do with beliefs and values. Different people believe different things. And what we believe influences what we do and what happens to us. We all have frameworks or 'metaprograms' (see page 121), through which we react to different contexts in life. Do we move towards or away from things to motivate ourselves, for example? Do we prefer global ideas or nitty gritty details? And so on. We don't all have the same metaprograms.

I say tomayto, you say tomahto!

We also differ in how we experience the world and how we represent 'reality' in our mind. We all see, hear, feel, smell and taste things externally and internally, but we do so in different ways and to different degrees.

In a piece of 'silly research', Virginia Satir found that there are more than 250 ways to wash up, depending on who is doing it and what they are using!

Implications

♦ Be aware that there are other ways of thinking about things and doing things that might be just as valid or effective as your ways. Acknowledge different students' 'maps' and use them to advantage to generate learning.

♦ Avoid guessing what other people's maps are: ask. You are not a mind-reader. Imposing other people's maps on them is as bad as imposing your own, if not worse.

♦ Be open to the fact that people are different from each other – and from you. As a 'teacher' among 'learners' you are potentially very powerful: be careful to offer – rather than impose – your own opinions and ideas.

♦ One way of learning is to try out other people's maps: encourage learners to find out how other people do things and see if they work for them too. (You could try it too.)

 DIFFERENT VIEWS OF THE SEA

How would the following people experience the sea? Write down the first thing that comes into your head.

♦ a fisherman

♦ a mermaid

♦ an artist

♦ a child

♦ an ice-cream vendor

♦ a computer scientist

Did you have trouble with the last one? Why? Was it because there is no obvious connection between a computer scientist and the sea? Were you making assumptions about how the other people 'should' view the sea? No doubt all of them experience the sea differently at different times, and similarly a computer scientist is likely to feel differently about it, depending on whether she's on holiday, writing a poem about it, or fighting for her life in a capsizing boat.

The point is that we must be aware that people experience the world in different ways. We must be careful not to jump to conclusions about what that experience is.

 YOUR MAP

What sort of map – a real map this time – would you choose to represent yourself and your life? A detailed wall chart of a country? A tiny geography book sketch? A world atlas? A fold-up road map? A sketch on the back of an envelope? What? How big is it? What condition is it in? New? Old? Well-cared-for?

Does the map you have chosen represent your life as it is or as you would like it to be? Is there a big difference between the two?

Think about other people you know. What kind of map would you choose to represent each of them?

What kind of map do you think they would choose to represent themselves?

Most countries place themselves at the centre of their map of the world.
So do most people.

 TRANSFER TO TEACHING

How could you use this activity with your students? What safeguards would you need to build in?

Asclepius and the Two Travellers

 Asclepius was once walking in the countryside outside Athens. At noon the sun was high in the sky and Asclepius had been walking since dawn. As the sun beat down, he became aware that he was feeling decidedly hot and thirsty. Then nearby he heard a most welcome sound – the sound of trickling water. He followed the sound and came across the source – a small stream. He sat down thankfully in the cool shade and gratefully rinsed his hands in the water. Just at this point where it rose out of the ground, it felt refreshingly cold, almost icy. He cupped his hands together, filled them with the pure water and raised it to his lips. Nothing had ever tasted so wonderful.

Just at that moment a traveller came by.

'Excuse me,' said the man, 'I'm going to Athens and I've never been there before. Have you any idea what it's like?'

'Where have you come from?' asked Asclepius.

'Piraeus,' said the man.

'Well, what's that like?' asked Asclepius.

'Oh it's a dreadful place,' said the man. 'Full of traffic and noise and dirt and unfriendly people. It's a terrible place.'

'Well, I expect you'll find Athens just the same,' said Asclepius.

'Oh dear,' said the man, and he walked slowly on his way.

Asclepius realised that he was feeling quite hungry after all his walking. Out of his pack he took the food he had brought with him. First there was a hunk of bread, freshly baked that morning. He took a deep breath and enjoyed the smell of it for a moment. Then white, sharp feta cheese made from his own goats' milk, and big black olives. And to follow, a large sweet juicy orange. His mouth was watering with anticipation, when he was interrupted by another traveller.

'Excuse me,' said the second man. 'I'm going to Athens and I've never been there before. Have you any idea what it's like?'

'Where have you come from?' asked Asclepius.

'Piraeus,' said the second man.

'Well, what's that like?' asked Asclepius.

'Oh it's a wonderful place,' said the man. 'Full of life and gaiety and colour and friendly people. It's a fantastic place.'

'Well, I expect you'll find Athens just the same,' said Asclepius.

'Oh good,' said the man, and he walked briskly on his way.

Asclepius smiled and bit into his bread. It was delicious.

Q

QUIZ – SENSORY STYLES

Which statements are true of you? Put a number in each box.

4 = always   3 = usually   2 = often   1 = occasionally   0 = never

Don't spend too long thinking about the answers, just write down the number which seems most appropriate, or most like your behaviour.

1 When you contact people, do you prefer
- ☐ (a) meeting face to face?
- ☐ (b) talking on the phone?
- ☐ (c) getting together to share an activity (walking, sports, etc)?

2 When you are angry, do you
- ☐ (a) go very quiet and seethe inwardly?
- ☐ (b) shout and let everyone know about it?
- ☐ (c) clench your fists, grit your teeth, storm off?

3 When you close your eyes to imagine something, do you naturally hold your head
- ☐ (a) up high?
- ☐ (b) slightly on one side?
- ☐ (c) down?

4 When you close your eyes and imagine something, do you
- ☐ (a) see clear, detailed pictures?
- ☐ (b) think in sounds or words?
- ☐ (c) get a feeling, perhaps with blurry images?

5 How is your memory? Do you tend to
- ☐ (a) forget names but remember faces?
- ☐ (b) remember names, words and numbers?
- ☐ (c) remember best the things you've done?

6 Is your room
- ☐ (a) tidy, nice to look at?
- ☐ (b) focused around the stereo?
- ☐ (c) arranged for comfort?

7 In your leisure time, do you prefer to
- ☐ (a) watch TV, read?
- ☐ (b) listen to music or a radio programme?
- ☐ (c) do something physical, eg go for a walk?

8 In conversation, do you
- ☐ (a) dislike either talking or listening for too long?
- ☐ (b) enjoy listening but get impatient to talk?
- ☐ (c) use a lot of gestures?

9 When you are forced to sit and wait, do you
- ☐ (a) look around, watch things?
- ☐ (b) talk to yourself or other people?
- ☐ (c) fidget, bite your nails?

10 When you are reading, do you
- ☐ (a) enjoy descriptive passages, imagine scenes clearly?
- ☐ (b) enjoy dialogue, hear the characters speaking?
- ☐ (c) prefer action stories, or tend not to read much?

11 What sort of clothes do you like wearing?
- ☐ (a) neat lines and good colours
- ☐ (b) don't really think about it
- ☐ (c) looser fitting, above all comfortable (eg baggy jogging bottoms)*

12 Is your voice
- ☐ (a) quite fast and high pitched?
- ☐ (b) rhythmical, and you tend to talk to yourself?
- ☐ (c) lower and slower?

---

* 'Baggy jogging bottoms' is not only what we like to wear, it's also one of our favourite tongue twisters.
Try saying 'baggy jogging bottoms' three times quickly and clearly!

QUIZ ANSWERS – SENSORY STYLES

Read these answers in relation to the information in **VAKOG 1 How we experience the world** and **VAKOG 2: How we represent the world** on the following pages.

These answers are just a guide and should not be taken too seriously. All the questions are generalisations and there will always be exceptions.

- (a) relates to visual
- (b) relates to auditory
- (c) relates to kinaesthetic

A score of 30+ in any one of the senses shows that you probably have a very strong preference for that sensory system. Make sure that when you are learning something new, you use methods and techniques which favour that sense. (See page 32) If you are presenting information to other people, make sure you use all three senses and not just the one which comes most naturally to you.

A score of 0-15 in any one sense shows that it is not very developed. Why not add to your repertoire as a teacher, learner and communicator by consciously using that sense more? Be careful not to omit techniques in this sense when helping other people learn.

A similar high score in all three senses shows a flexible approach and gives you more choices when learning, teaching and communicating. Remember to use them all and to continue adding techniques to all three.

If you have a similar low score in all three senses, what *are* you doing???

VAKOG 1: How we experience the world

We experience the world through our five senses or 'representational systems'. In NLP the five systems are called 'VAKOG' for short:

Visual	we look and see
Auditory	we hear and listen
Kinaesthetic	we feel externally (= tactile)
	we feel internally (= visceral or emotional)
	we feel movement (= psycho-motor)
Olfactory	we smell things
Gustatory	we taste

Unless we have physical or psychological problems, we all use all five systems, although the three most people use predominantly are V, A and K. While dogs and cats take in a great deal of information through the olfactory system, bats have a very well developed auditory system, and fish ... well, which one of the five senses do fish use predominantly?*

The systems we use to experience the world are called our **primary** representational systems. Depending to some extent on context, most people naturally tend to use one system more than the other two, or one system before the others, either when noticing things around them, or when learning something new. In NLP this is called the **preferred primary representational system**. There are some people who have such an extreme preference for one of the systems that they tend to 'translate' anything they experience into that system. There are people who 'feel' colours, or 'see' music or talk to themselves about everything that is happening, etc. Again, this is natural and most people can do the same if they think about it. (Think about it. It's fun!) And don't forget that some people have a very highly developed sense of smell – and presumably some go around tasting things a lot!

> "If the child is not learning the way you are teaching, then you must teach in the way the child learns."
>
> RITA DUNN

People who experience the world primarily **visually** like to take in information through their eyes. They like to see things written down, read books, look at pictures, diagrams and so on. They take notes (usually neatly) in order to look at them again.

People who experience the world primarily **auditorily** like to get information through their ears. They like to hear things being said, listen to cassettes, perhaps even have a chance to repeat things in their own head. They would rather record a lecture than take notes.

People who experience the world primarily **kinaesthetically** like to get information through their hands or bodies or emotions. They like to touch things, move their hands or feet, walk around the room. They also take notes, not necessarily to look at them again, but because the movement of their hand across the page helps them to absorb information. (Jane was very happy to discover this, as she had always felt vaguely guilty about writing pages of notes which she never looked at again.)

---

* kinaesthetic – fish sense vibration in the water

Implications

- If you know your preferred primary representational system, you can make sure you get your information in the right sort of way.

- But – the more the merrier! It's also good to develop those systems you tend to use less, because the more systems you learn and store something in, the better chance you have of remembering it. So if, for example, you are aware of being highly visual, work on enhancing your auditory and/or kinaesthetic systems. How? Well, one of the reasons Jane did a course in art history recently was to improve her visual acuity. Susan did a drawing course. They both plan to take singing lessons to build auditory acuity. And for fun too.

- The traditional classroom has focused primarily on writing and listening, which mainly favours people whose preferred system is visual or auditory. Students who are strongly kinaesthetic have tended to lose out academically, while continually being told to stop fidgeting and sit up straight!

- Your students will have different preferred primary representational systems or learning styles. You need to satisfy all of your students and not just the ones who happen to share your own preference. You can also help your students become more flexible in the systems they use and enhance the ones they use less. This means teaching in multi-sensory ways, using as many channels as you can as much of the time as possible: stimulate your students visually, auditorily and kinaesthetically – and olfactorily or gustatorily if you can!

- Improving auditory acuity will obviously be of great benefit to students' pronunciation when learning a foreign language.

- When you revise or recycle language, try to do it in all three representational systems – or at least in a different system from when you first presented it. Using the same stimulus will help them remember initially, but does not encourage them to transfer the learning to other situations.

TEACHING ACTIVITIES

Which of the following teaching activities favour the different representational preferences of the students? Write in the letter V, A or K against each activity.

1   Using lots of pictures, graphs, colour and shapes   _____
2   Using cassettes with varied voices, songs, music, rhythm and rhyme   _____
3   Having real objects for students to touch as they talk about them   _____
4   Oral drills (eg in the language laboratory)   _____
5   Decorating the classroom with pictures, students' work, etc   _____
6   Pausing when you speak from time to time to allow students
    to repeat what has been said (in their head or out loud)   _____
7   Allowing students to take notes   _____ & _____
8   Using mime and activities that get students moving   _____
9   Drama and role-play   _____
10 Giving an overview of what you are going to teach   _____
11 Practical project work   _____
12 Engaging students' feelings   _____

–––––––––––––––––––– SUGGESTED ANSWERS ––––––––––––––––––––

1 - V, 2 - A, 3 - K, 4 - A, 5 - V, 6 - A, 7 - V/K, 8 - K, 9 - K, 10 - V, 11 - K, 12 - K

EXPLORE YOUR TEACHING PREFERENCES

You're probably using a lot of the activities above already, even if you were not specifically aware of the different representational systems. The variety helps all students (for a change of pace and to make more links with new material) not just those who have a strong preference for one system. However, you might like to think back and list different teaching and learning activities you have done in class recently for presenting or practising information. Categorise them according to the VAK system (some activities may fall into one category, some into two and some into all three). Put ticks in the diagram to show the frequency of each type of activity – one tick for each time you did an activity (even if it was repeated).

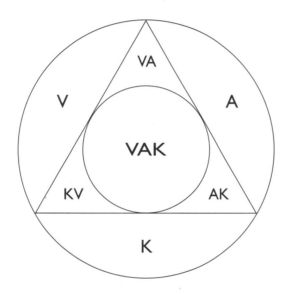

What have you learnt about your preferred teaching style? Can you plan activities which incorporate all three styles into your own teaching programme?

TEACHING TASKS

Just for practice, think about how you could make each of the following language teaching activities accessible in all three representational systems.*

- Introducing the structure 'can / can't'
- Correcting a variety of mistakes that many students are making
- Telling a story (listening comprehension)
- Exploiting / practising a dialogue from the textbook
- Writing a personal letter

---

* Suggested answers on page 139

Keep things in perspective

Remember, it isn't always possible to incorporate all representational systems into every activity you do and that's fine. It is a good idea, however, to try to get a balance in your lessons. And being aware of it is the first step.

Remember too that the aim of NLP is to give people more choices, not take them away; VAKOG is not about pigeon-holing people. The idea of a preferred system has sometimes been misrepresented as meaning that people operate through only one system. We operate with all five systems. It is simply that many of us find it easier to take in information first through one system. We just have to work a bit harder to get information through the others.

BE AN ARTIST

Improve your visual awareness by thinking like an artist.

♦ Look out of the window. You are an artistic photographer imprisoned in this room. Your next exhibition is called 'Views from my Window'. How many different and imaginative photographs can you take? In colour or black and white – long shot, wide angle, with a zoom, vertical, horizontal, turning the camera at an angle, …? Experiment. Look.

♦ Look around the room you're in now. How would you draw your surroundings? Which part would you choose to focus on? Look at the shapes, shadows and colours as an artist would. The table might be brown, but how does the colour differ when it's in shadow? What colour is it really when there's light falling on it? How many different shades of brown are there? You know that a box (or picture or window frame) has rectangular surfaces, but what shape is it from the angle you are looking from? Really look.

> If you find yourself saying 'But I can't draw …', try adding the word '… yet'.

♦ Try this technique for improving your drawing skills. Look at the teapot below. Now look at the shapes in the box where the teapot isn't! Draw the shapes around the teapot. You will find that by drawing the empty spaces you have also drawn the teapot, because they share a common boundary. Try the technique again by drawing the chair on page 21, or some objects around you.

Notice how you see things differently once you start thinking like an artist.

VAKOG 2: How we represent the world

As well as experiencing the external world through our senses (our primary system), we also use our senses to access information internally when we remember or imagine things. In NLP, this is called the **lead system.** Different people do this in different ways and many people tend to have a preferred representational system when they remember or imagine.

The preference in the lead system may or may not be the same as we have when we take in external information through our primary system. You might, for instance, experience the external world in a highly visual way and access information (think, remember things, create ideas) in pictures too. Or you might use two different systems. While Jane's preferred primary system is kinaesthetic, her preferred lead system is visual: when she recalls something she usually gets a picture first. The 'first' is important. As with our primary system, we do not use one system alone, we can use all five. We may tend to use one system first, but one or more of the others will usually follow, often fairly quickly. We get a picture, for example, and then almost immediately the sounds might come in and then we get a feeling, and so on.

To establish your preferred lead system, however, you need to identify the first system you normally use, the one which 'leads'. Sometimes this is very easy, but sometimes everything seems to happen at once and it's hard to isolate what happens first.

Some people actually do use two or more systems absolutely simultaneously. This is called synaesthesia. And some people do very strange and wonderful things. The Russian painter, Wassily Kandinsky, apparently saw sounds and heard colours in his head.

Just so you know

Not everyone in NLP makes a distinction between 'primary' and 'lead' representational systems, but we think it's a useful clarification of a fairly complex subject. External experience registers in the brain just as internal representation does, and we are frequently doing both almost simultaneously, so it's not always easy to identify exactly what's going on at any one time.

You might also read about a third representational system – our **reference system.** This is the system we use to double check – the system we use when someone asks us the question 'Are you sure?' Our preferred reference system may be the same as our primary or lead system, or it may be different. So if someone offers you a cup of tea, you may get a picture (of a cup of tea) which doesn't appeal (visual lead system) and say 'No, thank you.' If they say, 'Are you sure?', you may then get a feeling (of not needing anything to drink) which confirms your decision (kinaesthetic reference system).

THE LEAD VAK TEST:
READ AND IMAGINE

Follow each instruction in your mind and give yourself a mark:

0 = impossible   1 = difficult   2 = OK   3 = easy

__ SEE a kangaroo
__ SEE your front door
__ SEE your toothbrush
__ SEE a friend's face
__ SEE a plate of food
__ SEE a TV show …
__ WATCH the TV scene change

__ HEAR a song
__ HEAR rain
__ HEAR a fire alarm
__ HEAR a friend's voice
__ HEAR your own voice
__ HEAR birds singing …
__ HEAR the birdsong change to
  a call of alarm

__ FEEL excited
__ FEEL yourself swimming
__ FEEL grass under your feet
__ FEEL a cat* on your lap
__ FEEL hot
__ FEEL your fingers on a piano keyboard
__ FEEL your fingers playing a few notes

When you've done the test:

♦ Add up your scores for each sense: SEE ____ HEAR ____ FEEL ____

♦ Does the highest score correspond with what you think your preferred lead system is? How did you fare when it came to changing the scenes slightly in the last one of each section?

♦ Think of ways to enhance the systems you don't find so easy.

TRANSFER TO TEACHING

We use this as a reading or listening comprehension with students. They also enjoy comparing experiences afterwards too.

---

* If you don't like cats, think of something else: a rabbit? a child? Pavarotti?

 THINK ABOUT WHAT YOU
DO IN YOUR HEAD!

Take a sheet of paper and make five columns, like this:

SEE   HEAR   FEEL   SMELL   TASTE

Read each word in the box below and identify how you first represent it in your mind: Do you SEE the thing or SEE the word? Do you HEAR the sound the thing makes or HEAR the word being spoken? Do you FEEL the thing, either physically or emotionally? Do you SMELL it? Do you TASTE it? Write the word in the appropriate column.

Try to identify the very first thing you do. If you smell it, for example, are you sure that you don't get a quick image first? Don't think too long – you can probably represent almost anything in a variety of ways if you think about it long enough.

RAIN · SILK · ONION · COMPUTER · TELEPHONE · GARLIC ·
STORY BOOK · MOON · RIVER · GRASS · BUS · SAND · ROSE
· CHURCH · LEATHER · COFFEE · FISH · CAT · TRAIN · BABY ·
FRIEND · YOURSELF · YOUR COUNTRY · LONDON · POLITICS
· LEARNING ENGLISH · MATHS · LOVE · THE FUTURE

How did you get on? Did you have more words in one or two columns than in the others? Did the activity reinforce what you suspected about yourself or did you get some surprises?

This is a very tiny sample on which to base any firm conclusions, but it may confirm your intuitive sense of how you represent the world. Of course, for particular individuals some words may be context-dependent. Even though Jane tends to get pictures before anything else, there are many times when she doesn't. The word 'church', for example, immediately evokes the smell of incense, before she gets an image of the church itself.

 ## TRANSFER TO TEACHING

A 'column dictation' is a wonderful activity for integrating the four skills, with low teacher preparation and high student participation and motivation. You can use the same format for asking students to sort any items into relevant columns. This particular one helps students to think about how they represent things in their minds, in terms of which senses they use. It also highlights the fact that different people represent things in different ways: there is no one right way.

Students either read the words or listen to you reading them. In the follow-up discussion in groups of two, three or four, students can explain their experiences more precisely by asking and answering questions such as: 'What exactly did you see / hear / feel / smell / taste?'

Help – I can't do it!

After we've done guided fantasy and visualisation work with teachers and students, there's usually someone who secretly confesses some 'failing', such as 'not seeing proper pictures'. Here's the good news: *You cannot do this wrong!*

What is important (and fascinating) is to notice how your mind works. Everyone is different. Later we'll look at ways of 'changing your mind' and making it work in different ways. If you like the changes, you can keep them. If you don't, you can stay as you are.

When someone says they 'can't visualise', are they saying they have no imagination? Of course not. Everyone can image-ine or make some kind of image. The pictures may be blurry or merely a vague idea or sense of a picture, rather than the clear picture you get when you actually look through your eyes at the outside world. Maybe their imagination is strongly auditory or kinaesthetic. That's fine. That's how they visualise. What is interesting is that they are still able to answer questions about their 'pictures', even if they say they don't 'see' any! (See page 73)

It is possible to get clearer pictures. The more you practise, the more likely this is. It took Susan quite a long time (months) before she could get anything like a clear picture when she visualised – and her pictures are still a bit temperamental.

If you're having difficulties, try some or all of the following techniques. First, in your mind's eye, see a picture of the door to your house or flat.

- If your picture is blurry, peel off the top blurry picture and see if there's a clearer picture underneath.

- If you have no sense of a picture at all, get the image in a rep system other than visual and then use it as a bridge towards getting a picture (this is called 'mapping across'). For example:

  Can you hear the key going into the lock and the door opening? Can you get the feeling of what it's like to arrive home? Can you feel your hand on the door handle or turning the key in the lock? As you feel the key in your hand, going into the lock, you may begin to see the lock, and then the door ...

- If you can't picture the real image, try picturing a photograph of the image. (Susan's mind will often fall for that one.)

- Fake it. Pretend you can visualise. If you could see a picture of your door, what would it be like?

- Work with what you get. Take pride in the mind you've got. It's done pretty well for you so far!

Now see that door again, and take the appropriate action if the door doesn't appear before you.

Eye movements

Next time you are asking students to imagine, watch their eye movements. For example, you ask them to imagine a huge bonfire. Make sure they have a really clear sense of being there and experiencing the bonfire fully. Then tell certain students that you think you can read how their mind was working.

Those people who are looking up to the right or to the left, almost certainly have a clear picture. People whose heads are bent slightly to the side and whose eyes are level and looking to one side are probably hearing the crackle of the flames. People with bent heads looking down are feeling – maybe the heat of the flames, or maybe they have an emotional reaction to the bonfire. Try it. Or try it for yourself.

There is a correlation between the representational system a person is using and their eye movements. The basic model is this:

- If a person's eyes look to their left they are remembering something (the word we use is recall). It is often related to the past.

- If they go to their right, the person is imagining or inventing something (construct). This might be related to the future.

- If they go up, the person is visualising, making pictures.

- If they go left or right towards the ears, they are listening to sounds or words.

- If they look down, they are feeling kinaesthetically (emotionally or physically).

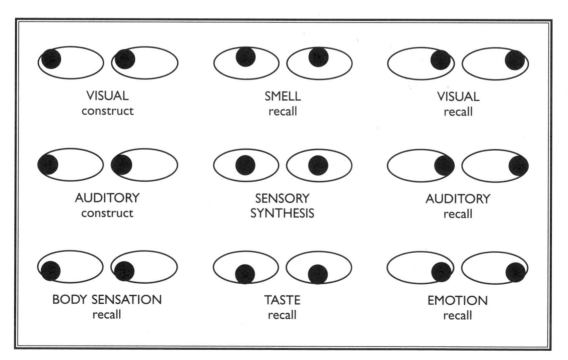

THE DEVORE MODEL OF EYESCAN PATTERNS

(The eyes as seen by someone else)

The significance of eye movements has been known about since the sixties and the model most often used in NLP is the one that Grinder and Bandler described in *Frogs into Princes* in 1979. The more recent model we use here is by Stephen Devore, and includes smell, taste and 'sensory synthesis'. The latter is when a person is using more than one rep system and – typically – gazing into the middle distance with slightly out-of-focus eyes.

A model is only a model. It's very useful to know what the standard is, but not everyone will fit into it exactly. Be prepared for people to deviate a little – or a lot. It may or *may not* be connected with left and right-handedness. However, even though someone's pattern may be totally different from the ones shown here, it will almost certainly be consistent. Be observant, experiment, tell people what you're doing and ask them what's going on in their head.

How do you look?

Experiment with your own eye movements. Do the Lead VAK Test from page 36 again and notice where your eyes go. Remember that your recall is likely to be to your left and your construct to the right. Make notes about your experience.

You may find that your eyes move around a lot. In this case, the final position is usually where you have 'found' your image and the first position was where you first looked. This may indicate a rep system preference.

If you have trouble finding any of the pictures, sounds or feelings, try moving your eyes consciously to where the model suggest you will find them. Does that make it easier? If it does, use the strategy to help you remember or imagine in the future. And you can also use the strategy in class to help your students.

How do they look?

Do the previous activity with a friend. Watch their eyes and note the movements. Discuss what they were doing in their mind and compare it with what you saw.

Ask them to do the same for you. Compare what they see with what you experienced when you did the activity yourself.

Try out the activity with other friends and with students.

After a while if you use the same VAK test too often, all your eye movements will begin to indicate 'recall' as you remember the last time you did the test! Make up some variations, eg alligator for kangaroo, relative's face for friend's face, church bell, pop group, etc. If students do this activity, making up variations for the various categories is also good vocabulary practice.

Begin to notice people's eye movements generally. This isn't always easy when you are deep in conversation – you may forget to listen to what people are saying! It is easy to practise when you're watching an interview on television though, or when people around you are having a conversation that you're not involved in. And you do need to practise. Most people are not used to looking for these clues. Once you start, not only does it become totally fascinating, you understand people and can get on with them a lot better too.

NLP SPELLING TECHNIQUE

Spelling phonetically is easy in phonetic languages. English is not a phonetic language, so people (even native speakers) who use an auditory phonetic approach, tend to be poor spellers. (The word 'phonetic' isn't even spelt how it sounds.)

Good spellers in English are people who visualise the word (eyes looking up). They often then check how it feels kinaesthetically to write the word. You can teach the technique to people who do not naturally spell well, and we find it is also very effective for foreign students learning the written form of new vocabulary.

The steps are:

1 Hold a card up high with the word on it, or write it high on the board, so that students have to look up to see it.

2 Tell the students consciously to blink their eyes to take a mental photograph of the word.

3 They close their eyes and picture the word clearly, looking up inside their heads to see the 'photograph' they have just taken.

4 They write down the word from memory.

5 Repeat 1-4 as often as necessary until students know the word. If necessary break long words into shorter sections, or ask students to imagine any problem parts bigger. They can also try making the whole word bigger in their heads.

6 To prove their success, ask them to visualise the word and then spell it backwards by 'reading' the letters from their heads. This is only possible if they can 'see' it.

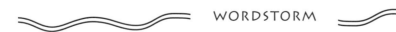 WORDSTORM

Think back over the last two sections and write down any words which will help you remember the key points. (See page 24)

Sensory language

The language people use, like their eye movements, can show which representational system they are using at a particular moment.

For example, while people are experiencing or representing visually, they tend to use **visual language** – literally. They say things like: *'I see what you mean'* or *'I get the picture'* or *'I need a different perspective on that.'*

While people are experiencing or representing auditorily, they tend to use **auditory language** such as: *'That doesn't sound right'* or *'I hear what you're saying but …'* or *'His name rings a bell.'*

While people are experiencing or representing **kinaesthetically,** they might say something like: *'I feel it's wrong'* or *'That doesn't grab me'* or *'I can't quite grasp that idea.'*

And of course there is **olfactory** and **gustatory language** too: *'That's a bit fishy'*, *'I don't like the smell of this'*, *'It's left a bad taste in my mouth.'*

These sensory-specific words are often referred to in NLP as **predicates.**

SORT AND ADD

Are these words and expressions visual, auditory, kinaesthetic, olfactory, gustatory or neutral (ie unspecified representational system)? Write **V, A, K, O, G** or **N** next to each of them. Remember you are considering the literal meaning of the words this time, and not your own interpretation.*

see ___	hear ___	feel ___	think ___	smell ___
taste ___	sound ___	grasp ___	picture ___	focus ___
heavy ___	fit ___	tone ___	handle ___	believe ___
experience ___	grab ___	odour ___	describe ___	harmony ___
look at ___	tune in ___	understand ___	point of view ___	

That rings a bell! ___   I'm getting cold feet about this. ___
It's a piece of cake! ___   See it from my perspective. ___
My mind's gone blank! ___   She knows how to push his buttons. ___
Give them the cold shoulder. ___   It's not just a bit fishy; it stinks! ___
We're not singing the same tune. ___   Wonderful! ___   Smashing! ___
Cool! ___   Brilliant! ___   It's OK. ___

THINK

Before you read on, brainstorm words and phases to add to each of the six categories. Which category do you find easiest? Why?

---

* Compare your answers with our suggestions on the following pages. If you tended to put 'neutral' words into a specific system, or your answers vary greatly from ours, this may be additional evidence of a strong sensory preference on your part.

Just so you know

In addition to the distinction between lead, primary and reference representational systems, some people in NLP make a further distinction by saying that predicates indicate our primary system, and eye movements indicate our lead system. Well … we tried keeping to that but we found that it just doesn't work in our experience. So our approach is that both language and eye movements are useful clues as to how a person is either experiencing or representing the world.

We tried to do something we hadn't seen before, which was to list equivalent words and phrases for each of the senses, but we soon discovered that in many cases there is no direct equivalent. However, some very common words and phrases do have an equivalent (or approximate equivalent) in all systems and we have noticed that these are often a very reliable indicator of the system a person is using. For words and phrases without an equivalent, a specific meaning can best, or only, be expressed in one system rather than another.

There is a lot more research to be done in this area. For example, do we learn specific idioms and patterns of speech from significant other people in our lives – parents or teachers, perhaps? Maybe we use a particular idiom in a foreign language because it is the only one we know!

We invite you to explore this area, both in English and in your own language. Notice what sort of language you yourself use and how this reflects the way you are thinking. Notice what others say and how they say it. If appropriate, check out with them how they were representing ideas in their mind at that moment.

At the very least this is an alternative, fun way of mining a rich seam of vocabulary and idioms. The whole area of VAKOG gives rise to a lot of interesting language based on the senses. Many of the words, particularly the kinaesthetic ones, tie in very well with language linked to mind and body. (See page 20) Consider the following too:

- The five senses: *sight (seeing), hearing, touch (feeling), smell, taste*

- The corresponding parts of the body: *eyes, ears, skin / fingers* (plus *gut* and *heart* for emotions?), *nose, tongue*

- The corresponding verbs: *see (watch, look at), hear (listen to), touch / feel, smell, taste.* Notice how many are intransitive as well as transitive.*

- The corresponding descriptive phrases: *looks* + adjective, *looks like* + noun, *looks as if* + verb phrase (and similar constructions with *sounds, feels, tastes* and *smells*)

- Adjectives to describe sights, sounds feelings (tactile and emotional), smells and tastes. Notice how few specific ways there are of describing smell and taste compared to the other three. We very quickly have to revert to comparing smells and tastes to other things, eg *It tastes lemony. It smells like newly-baked bread.*

- Associated expressions and idioms (See the following pages)

---

* which leads us to that well-known example of English humour:
  'I say, I say, I say, my dog's got no nose.' 'No nose? How does it smell?' 'Terrible.'

 EQUIVALENCE

Can you match these neutral expressions with the corresponding expressions below which relate to the different senses?*

a I don't understand.

b I'm beginning to understand.

c I don't like that.

d We disagree.

e My opinion is …

f I understand.

g Let me explain.

h I'm against …

i I've had an idea.

j We understand each other.

k What are you concentrating on?

l Consider this.

Visual

1 I can picture that clearly.

2 I can't quite see it.

3 We see things the same way.

4 We don't see eye to eye.

5 Look at it this way.

6 It's becoming clear to me.

7 Something just flashed through my mind. / It's just dawned on me.

8 Let me paint a detailed picture.

9 I take a dim view of that.

10 What are you focusing on?

11 I've got a blind spot about …

12 My viewpoint is …
    My point of view is …

Auditory

I hear what you are saying

It's all Greek to me

We speak the same language

We're on different wavelengths.

Listen to this …

It's beginning to make sense.

I've just clicked.

Let me spell it out for you.
Let me tell you word for word.

That's uncalled for.

What are you stressing?

I'm deaf to …

–

Kinaesthetic

I catch your drift.

I'm not with you.

We're close in lots of ways.

We just don't connect.

Let me run this by you …

I'm on the right track.
I'm getting there.

It's just struck me.
I've made a connection.

Let me take you through it step by step.
Let me walk you through it.

That doesn't grab me.

What are you getting at?

I'm closed to / not open to …

My standpoint is …
Where I stand is …

Predicates

Look out for words or expressions which are specific to one representational system when you or other people use them. When you are teaching, use a good cross-section of predicates from all rep systems, as well as using neutral words that students can experience in any system they choose. The selection below will help you to know what to look for.

NEUTRAL

Nouns

thing, experience, thought, knowledge, understanding, description, representation, memory, belief

Verbs

think, believe, understand, remember, know, experience, describe, represent, explain, agree, disagree, concentrate, comprehend, consider

Adjectives

great, wonderful, excellent, OK, easy

VISUAL

Nouns

picture, image, point of view, viewpoint, perspective, focus, insight, horizon, scene, sight, glimpse

Verbs

see, look at, show, picture, focus, illustrate, visualise, reflect, dazzle, glance at, perceive, gaze

Adjectives

blinded, blank, hazy, blurred, revealing, bright, graphic, short-sighted, brilliant, clear,* lucid, opaque

Expressions/idioms

My mind's gone blank. The future looks dim. Let's look closely at this. To shed some light on something. My view is a bit coloured. It appears that …

AUDITORY

Nouns

sound, tune, tone, voice, volume, discord, harmony, echo, accent

Verbs

hear, listen to, tell, say, speak, talk, shout, stress,* harmonize, tune in, amplify, ring, accentuate

Adjectives

deaf, dumbfounded, out of tune, off key, flat, sharp, speechless, loud, clear,* smashing*

Expressions/idioms

That rings a bell. To sing the same tune. That's music to my ears. I hear you loud and clear. What a lot of mumbo jumbo. That strikes a chord. Give/get an earful. I'm all ears.

---

* indicates words which appear in more than one rep system

KINAESTHETIC

Nouns

feeling, sensation, stress,* pressure, temperature, gut reactions, emotion, weight, attitude, posture

Verbs

feel, touch, connect, move, bear, support, grab, hold, sting, grasp, fit, catch

Adjectives

closed, stunned, heavy, hard, tangible, cold, hot, cool, knocked out, smashing,* sensational, comfortable, uncomfortable

Expressions/idioms

Give someone the cold shoulder. To get cold feet about something. To push someone's buttons. To wind someone round your little finger. He's a pain in the neck/arse. I'm going/falling to pieces. I feel it in my bones. I'm getting cold feet about this. I'm stuck/bogged down. That fits with my experience. I can't get a grip/handle on that. Give someone a rough ride. I can't put my finger on it. You cramp my style. Carpe diem (Latin) = seize the day / moment. Stick your neck out. Go over the same ground. Tread carefully. Blow hot and cold. Have an axe to grind. Meet me halfway.

OLFACTORY/GUSTATORY

Nouns

smell, aroma, perfume, odour, whiff, flavour, taste

Verbs

sniff, breathe in, stink, savour

Adjectives

fishy, stale, pungent, sour, sweet, bitter, acid, smelly, tasty, delicious

Expressions/idioms

It's a piece of cake! To have a good nose for something. To sniff out.

 TRANSFER TO TEACHING

Choose small groups of words or expressions for students to sort into the relevant VAKOG categories as a way of building vocabulary

There is no failure, only feedback

There is a story about Thomas Edison that goes something like this: When someone commented to Edison that he failed 1,999 times before he eventually managed to invent the light bulb, he replied, 'Nonsense, it was a 2,000 step process!'

When things don't go the way I want them to go, it does not mean that I am a complete and utter failure. When things don't go the way I want them to go, collapsing in a heap and moaning for hours or days on end is usually not very helpful, nor is it likely to make me happier (at least, not in the long-term). When things don't go the way I want them to go, the most useful way to respond, however bad I feel, is to ask myself, 'What did I learn from that? How can I do it differently next time so that it won't happen again, so that something different will happen?' This is not to say that I refuse to take responsibility for making a mistake that affects other people or that I minimise such events. What it means is that I accept responsibility, I do all I can to make amends, and ... I move on with new wisdom.

:::::::::::::::::::::::::::::::::::: Implications :::::::::::::::::::::::::::::::::::::

◆ Considering mistakes as a source of learning doesn't always come easily and often needs some practice. If this is not your normal way of thinking, try it out and see if it helps.

◆ Don't be too harsh on yourself, too self-critical. It's OK to make mistakes. We all do. And if we didn't, we'd never change or improve. Learn to equate making a mistake with making progress. Create a safe atmosphere in the classroom where it's fine for learners to take risks, make mistakes and get things wrong.

◆ The most successful learners are those who jump right in and have a go, unafraid of making mistakes – or of making a fool of themselves! Mistakes are positive evidence that

IT'S OK	
to try things out	to take time out
to ask questions	not to know
to feel unsure	to practise
to let your mind wander	to ask for help again – and again
to daydream	to make mistakes
to ask for help	to check your understanding
to experiment	

Class notice

learners are experimenting and ... changing. Be pleased. Help them to see mistakes in this way too, and to learn from them. Help them to welcome feedback and even actively to seek it, so that real learning takes place.

◆ Learners need constructive feedback to know what they could do differently. Focus on the solution rather than the problem. Constructive feedback needs to be at the level of behaviour rather than identity: 'You did this and this. Perhaps you could do this and this next time?' (Not: 'You aren't very good at X ...')

◆ See mistakes as useful feedback for your teaching! Concentrate less on the mistake itself than on the reason for making it.

Incidentally, Thomas Edison lived by his beliefs in relation to others too. When he finally invented a light bulb that worked, he gave the only one in existence to his assistant, who dropped it! After many hours of painstaking work, he managed to recreate a second prototype, which he immediately handed to the same assistant.

IN SPITE OF FAILURE – BECAUSE OF FAILURE

Time yourself on this task. Get paper and pencil and a clock or watch ready before you start. You have exactly one minute to write down answers to each of the following questions. Ready? Begin.

1 Write quick notes on how you feel about failure and mistakes.

2 Write down everything you learnt to do before the age of 10.

3 Write down everything you have ever learnt to do without making a mistake.

4 Write down any successes that wouldn't have happened if you hadn't made a mistake, or if you hadn't 'failed' at something.

5 Write down the most important lessons you have learnt because of failure or mistakes.

6 Write quick notes on how you feel about failure and mistakes.

SILLY VOICES

You know that voice in your head? The one that reminds you how stupid you are and what a failure you are. Yes, that one. Well, stop it. Change its tone. Make it deep and husky and seductive. 'You are sooooooo stupid, you gorgeous thing.' Make it a little high mousy squeak – or a deep low growl. Very quick – or very very slow. Then try Bugs Bunny or some other crazy cartoon character. Whatever you do, don't ever believe it or take it seriously again!

Robert the Bruce and the Spider

One of Scotland's greatest heroes is Robert the Bruce, who became King of Scotland almost seven hundred years ago. It was a time when Scotland and England were always at war because the English wanted the Scottish throne. The story goes that the English invaded Scotland and defeated the Scots. So Robert the Bruce had to escape to the Highlands and hide in a cave. It looked like the end for Scotland as an independent country and the end of his dream. Everything seemed hopeless. Sitting in his cave, he was on the point of giving up, when he saw a spider.

The spider was trying to spin its web across a gap in the rocks, but the web broke and the spider fell. The spider started building its web again. The web broke again and the spider fell again. It tried again. And failed again. It kept on trying and it kept on failing, again and again and again. Until finally it

succeeded. It built a perfect web.

Robert the Bruce learned a lesson from that spider. He decided to act. At a moment when England was ruled by a weak king, Edward II, he formed an army and led it against the English. In 1314, at Bannockburn, the Scottish army defeated the English army in the greatest victory the Scots ever won against the English.

Reframing: Changing words, changing minds

"Language, the loaded weapon" Dwight Bolinger

The words we use have a tremendous influence. When we label things by assigning a word to them, we fix them. And to a certain extent we fix our response to them too. If, for example, I call something 'a problem', then my attitude to it is determined: I am set to deal with something negative and I respond in a certain way. If I call it instead 'a challenge': I am set to deal with something new and exciting and I respond in a very different way.

> Did you know that the Chinese symbol for 'crisis' includes a symbol which means 'opportunity'?

One of the ways in which NLP consciously uses language is to rename or re-label things in order to alter our perception of them. We can give otherwise negative things a positive connotation, thereby giving us more choice of how to respond. This process is known as **reframing.**

Here are some more examples:

mistake	becomes	*lesson*
ending	becomes	*new beginning*
terrorist	becomes	*freedom fighter*

You'll find many more in the newspapers, especially in 'politician-speak'. That's why political parties employ 'spin doctors' to put a favourable interpretation on events.

Can you think of some **reframes** for the following words? Your suggestions will not be precise synonyms, but then that's the point! Change the way you think about something by changing what you call it, in order to change what you do about it.

aggressive	*disruptive*	*boring*	*timid*	*arrogant*
impatient	*cry-baby*	*coward*	*busy-body*	*crisis**

Make a list of some of the negative things you say to yourself and write a reframe next to each one. Does that change how you feel about them?

Listen out for negative labels and think of positive reframes for them even if you don't actually use them at the time. For example:

S *I'm such a coward.*   T *You're just being cautious.*
S *I'm so slow.*   T *You're taking your time/being thorough.*

———————————— SUGGESTED ANSWERS ————————————

* assertive, enthusiastic, calm, reflective, confident, keen, sensitive, cautious, looking to help, opportunity

How could you respond to these students to help them rethink their statement?*

S1 *My questions are holding everyone up.*

S2 *I don't get enough attention from the teacher.*

S3 *I keep on making mistakes.*

S4 *I'm too old.*

S5 *I'm hopeless at remembering people's names.*

S6 *I'm always bottom of the class.*

By the way ...

Feel OK about not coming up with a brilliant reframe on the spur of the moment. We have often thought of really good ones several hours – or even several days – after the event! Just keep practising and the times when you get it right at the right time will get more and more frequent.

There will, of course, be times when reframing is neither useful nor desirable. When someone is not being 'assertive', for example, but they are actually being 'aggressive', and you want to tell them so! Or when a 'mistake' is, quite frankly, a 'mistake'. If in doubt, ask yourself what you want to achieve ... and act accordingly.

 TRANSFER TO TEACHING

♦ Asking students to reframe negative adjectives can give rise to productive discussion of their precise meanings.

♦ Ask them to collect negative statements they make and hear others making – in any language, as long as they present them to you in English. The group can then compare possible reframes.

♦ Looking for 'politician-speak' in newspapers can be a very productive source of discussion, vocabulary and reading practice.

────────────── SUGGESTED ANSWERS ──────────────

* 1 My questions are getting us all to think. 2 He trusts me to get on with my work. 3 If I didn't make mistakes, I wouldn't be trying. 4 I have a lot of experience. 5 I do remember important things about people. 6 I can make more progress than anyone.

The map becomes the territory

If you lived in a magic world where everything you imagined would come true, how differently would you use your imagination? You do live in a magic world.

This NLP presupposition is all about the power of belief and about self-fulfilling prophecy. If you believe something to be true, you make it true. This is so both for positive, enabling beliefs and for negative beliefs that are limiting.

"Whether you think you can, or think you can't ... you're right!"

HENRY FORD

If you go around telling yourself that you can't remember names – as Jane has done for years – what do you think happens? Conversely, think about the power of saying 'I can do this.'

Two comparable classes were chosen for an experiment. One teacher was told she had exceptionally gifted children – the other that she had the duds. At the end of the year all the students in the 'gifted' class scored significantly higher in exams. The only difference was in the teachers' expectations.

Whenever you feel like saying 'Yes, but …', try saying instead 'Yes, and …'

What expectations do you have of your students, collectively or individually? Do you find that they live up (or sometimes down) to your expectations? Most of them do. Try using this power positively. Imagine that all your students are the intelligent, bright people who are destined to become world leaders and experts in their chosen field. Now try behaving towards them as if this were true. And try having similar expectations of yourself.

In the 1920s it was fashionable to repeat Emil Coué's sentence regularly to improve physical and mental health and well-being. You might like to try it:

Every day and in every way I am getting better and better.

:::::::::::::::::::::::::::::::::::: **Implications** ::::::::::::::::::::::::::::::::::::

- Give yourself (and others) positive messages, rather than negative ones.
- Help others to believe they can do things – that they can learn, for instance.
- Acknowledge what people are doing right instead of criticising what they are doing wrong. Always give positive feedback before suggestions for improvement.
- Building self-esteem in yourself as a teacher and your students as learners will improve learning.

Work towards success

Our teachers always told us to underline the words we didn't understand. Even when we subsequently did understand them, we were forever reminded of our previous limitations.

We encourage our students to underline or highlight the words they do understand. As they learn more, they literally fill in the gaps and underline more. They are working towards success.

 CHUCK OUT YOUR
LIMITING BELIEFS

Make a list of things that you think you can't do or are no good at – that you would really like to do or be good at. Some examples might be:

I can't understand computers.

I'm no good at maths.

I can't draw.

Make sure that your *'I can't …'* is not an *'I don't want to …'*, but rather some sort of limiting belief that you could usefully do without.

Rewrite your list in the form *'I can … if I choose to'*, or *'I can't … yet'*

for example:

I can understand computers if I choose to.

I can't draw yet.

Take the first list, screw it up and throw it in the waste paper basket. Good riddance!

Keep your new list handy, or pin it up on your wall. Now go and celebrate!

Well done!

 ### TRANSFER TO TEACHING

- If students work in small groups it helps them to think of examples of things they think they are no good at, and to identify which are based on limiting beliefs. This activity is a good balance between written and oral practice.
- The positive effect is stronger if you make a ceremony of throwing away the I can'ts, which can each be written on a separate piece of paper. Ask students to stand around the wastepaper basket. They then each look at one of their statements, screw it up and throw it into the basket, waving and saying 'Goodbye!' as they do so. Then they stand quietly and mentally reframe each negative statement as an affirming statement. Repeat until all the papers are in the bin. Then invite students to share one of their new affirmations with the class while others listen respectfully.

The Drought

*O*nce, *in a faraway country there was a drought. There had been no rain for days. No rain for weeks. No rain for months. And the land was dry, dry, dry. And hard and cracked and brown and dusty. And the sun beat down relentlessly. And the heat was unbearable. Like living in an oven. Impossible to breathe. And everywhere the dust. On the ground. In the air. On your skin. In your eyes. In your throat. Suffocating dust.*

And the plants were dying. Changing from green through yellow to brown, they withered and died. And the animals were starving: the cattle, the sheep, the pigs, the goats – getting thinner and thinner and thinner … and dying. And the people were starving too, for there was nothing to eat.

And the drought went on and on and on.

So one day, all the men went into the temple to pray for rain. In the sweltering heat, they got down on their knees on the hard, dusty ground and they prayed and they prayed and they prayed for rain. But still there was no rain.

And so another day, all the women went into the temple to pray for rain. In the sweltering heat, they got down on their knees on the hard, dusty ground and they prayed and they prayed and they prayed for rain. But still there was no rain.

And then one day, a little girl went up the steps to the temple. She was about nine and she was wearing a dirty yellow dress that was torn. Her feet were bare and her legs and arms were dusty. Her long hair was tangled and in a mess. There was dirt on her face. And up she went, up the steps of the temple, to pray for rain. But do you know what she had with her? She had with her an umbrella. Not a posh umbrella. A scruffy old broken umbrella. But an umbrella just the same. And she skipped into the temple and got down on her knees and put her umbrella on the ground beside her and she prayed and she prayed and she prayed for rain.

And do you know what? When she came out of the temple, it was raining.

Accentuate the positive

Whatever you do, don't think about a hippo on a trampoline.

What are you doing? You're thinking about a hippo on a trampoline, aren't you?

That's the problem with language! It brings things to our attention – and that little word 'not' is overlooked. Once we've heard the words, we can't un-hear them. That's why trial lawyers make the statements that the judge orders the jury to ignore. The jury can't ignore them.

Imagine you're walking through a jungle and come across a ferocious-looking, spear-carrying tribal warrior. You obviously don't speak the same language and you're going to die unless in the next 60 seconds you can mime the message: 'I don't want to kill you.' You've got 60 seconds, starting NOW.

Sorry. You're dead. You had a spear through your heart before you got round to miming the 'not' part of the message.

At a more everyday level, what is likely to happen in the following situations?

Me to myself: *I mustn't forget my umbrella.*

You to friend: *Don't forget your key!*

Mother to child: *Don't go near the water. I said, don't go near … Don't fall in! Now look what you've done. I told you not to go near the water!*

What positive outcomes were the speakers trying to achieve? Rephrase the instructions to give the speakers a better chance of achieving the desired effect.*

Apparently our non-conscious mind operates very much like a ferocious tribesman or a young child. It just doesn't understand the word not. According to Noam Chomsky's Transformational Grammar, the negative is not present in the *deep structure* meaning, but only in the transformations which change it into *surface structure* communications. Whatever the reason, it seems to be true that when you're speaking to yourself or to others, a positive message will be much more effective than a negative one. If you do use a negative instruction – often out of habit, but sometimes for emphasis – use a positive one alongside it.

So, with students, how could you rephrase these instructions so that they have the desired effect?**

       Don't fidget.   Don't look.   Don't talk.   Don't be late.   Don't try too hard.

Make a list of other instructions that are relevant to the classroom and make sure they are written positively.

POSITIVE – NEGATIVE TRANSFER

Put 50 toothpicks into your left hand pocket. Every time you have a negative thought, transfer one to your right-hand pocket.

The average person transfers all 50 toothpicks within 15 minutes!

Now try transferring the toothpicks back to your left pocket every time you have a positive thought. How quickly can you transfer them this time?

"You've got to ac–cent–tchu–ate the positive,
eliminate the negative.
Latch onto the affirmative.
Don't mess with Mr In–between."

POPULAR SONG

───────────── SUGGESTED ANSWERS ─────────────

  *   I must remember my umbrella. Remember your key. Walk on the path near where the big boys are playing football.

**   Keep still. Shut your eyes. Keep quiet. Be on time. Take it easy./Relax.

Brer Rabbit and the Bramble Patch

For once Brer Rabbit had been caught by Brer Fox. He was stuck fast to a sort of doll Brer Fox had made out of straw and tar and Brer Fox was very, very pleased with himself.

'Well I reckon I've got you this time,' said Brer Fox. 'You're looking very stuck up, if I might say so.' And he laughed and laughed until he almost split his sides. When he could talk again, he said, 'Now you just wait there while I go and light a fire ready for my Brer Rabbit barbecue!'

Brer Rabbit thought hard and he thought quickly and he said, in a thoughtful sort of voice, 'Well, if I've got to go, I think I'd rather go tasting of delicious barbecue sauce than be thrown into that bramble patch over there. Please, please don't throw me into that bramble patch.'

Brer Fox was quite surprised. He had expected Brer Rabbit to be terrified at the thought of being cooked on a fire.

'Hmm,' he said. 'It's a lot of trouble to light a fire. Maybe I'll just hang you from that tree over there.'

'You hang me just as high as you please,' said Brer Rabbit, 'but please, please don't throw me into that bramble patch.'

'Shucks,' said Brer Fox. 'I don't seem to have any rope with me. I guess I'll just have to drown you.'

'Yep, fine,' said Brer Rabbit. 'Drown me as deep as you like. But please, please don't throw me into that bramble patch.'

'Sorry. There doesn't seem to be any water round here,' said Brer Fox. 'There ain't nothing for it but to skin you alive.'

'Yes. Skin me alive. Scratch my eyes out. Pull off my ears. Anything. But please, please don't throw me into that bramble patch.'

Well Brer Fox wanted to hurt Brer Rabbit just as much as he possibly could, so he picked him up by his hind legs and swung him once, twice, three times round his head, and then threw him right into the thickest part of the bramble patch. And then he waited for the howls of pain.

And he waited.

But there were no howls of pain.

And just when he thought Brer Rabbit must be good and dead for sure, he suddenly heard a cry from the hillside.

'Yoo hoo. Brer Fox. Over here!'

There was Brer Rabbit sitting on the hillside as bold as bold could be, and Brer Fox understood that he'd been well and truly tricked.

'I was born and raised in that bramble patch, Brer Fox,' said Brer Rabbit. 'Born and raised in that bramble patch!'

Outcomes: knowing where you're going

Once you realise that you *can* achieve what you want to achieve, you need to be clear what you want. It is very difficult to move towards your goals until you have some, be they personal or professional, short or long-term.

Setting well-formed outcomes – one of the four pillars of NLP – is the crucial first step in the Basic Action Model. (See page 17) Once you know what it is you want, you can begin to imagine what it would be like, to rehearse it in your mind and to think about what steps you need to take. Then you can begin to move towards it. You have, in fact, already begun to move towards it.

Dreams

It's hard to talk about goals without also talking about dreams. And Walt Disney. Why Walt Disney? Well, Walt Disney was very creative and very successful. He was a dreamer. Walt Disney said: 'Before you plan, you need your dream to be there.' And his was.

"Cherish your visions and your dreams as they are the children of your soul, the blueprints of your ultimate achievements."

NAPOLEON HILL

Walt Disney would have a dream, and he would have a plan of how to get to that dream. He would invite people to criticise his plan and suggest improvements so he could reach his dream. But there was one thing the critics were not allowed to do. They were never, ever allowed to question the dream itself. The dream was sacrosanct.

'Well, of course,' perhaps you're saying, 'That's what we all do.'

Is it? I don't think so. Many of us start off with a dream and make plans on how to get there. But when we don't seem to be getting closer, instead of changing our plans, we change our dream. We reduce it in size to make it more attainable. And we often tend to end up with something mediocre because we think that it's more realistic, more reasonable.

Change your plan. Keep your dream.

:: **Implications** ::

◆ If you want to reach your goals, have some.

◆ Have classroom outcomes for yourself and your students. Share your outcomes with the students: knowing where they're going helps them to learn.

◆ Help your students to set their own outcomes.

◆ Dream – and encourage your students to dream.

◆ Break down big outcomes into smaller, more easily achievable ones.

◆ Remember: The longest journey starts with a single step.

Present state and desired state

A helpful way to start thinking about outcomes is to think in terms of **Present State**, **Desired State** and **Action** to link the two. Our **Present State** is where we are now, our current situation. Our **Desired State** is where we want to be. If these two states are the same, then we have what we want and we don't need to change anything. We are happy!

"Choice, not chance, determines destiny."

ANON

Very often, however, these two states are different and we want to take **action** to change our present state into our desired state. The big question is How? It's a question we don't always find easy to answer. One thing that can help us to find answers, however, is to stop focusing on the present 'problem' and what's wrong, and start concentrating on the desired 'solution' and what would be right.

 DOODLE A LINK

1 Take a sheet of paper, place it horizontally and divide it into 3 sections like this:

Present State	Action	Desired State

2 Think of a situation in your life that you would like to change. For your first attempt, you might like to choose a small or medium-sized 'problem'. How about something in your professional life?

3 Doodle a representation of this situation (your Present State) in the left-hand section. Use different colours if they seem appropriate.

Doodling is very much a non-conscious, going-with-the-flow, see-what-comes-up activity which often gives very interesting insights. If, however, you would rather draw something more consciously, that's fine.

4 Think of what you would like instead of your present situation.

5 Doodle (or draw) a representation of your Desired State on the right.

6 Now comes the interesting bit! Doodle (or draw) something – anything – in the centre which links the left and right sections. This represents your Action.

7 Now just sit awhile and look at the three doodles (or drawings). What do you learn? In particular, look at what action the centre section suggests.

8 How soon can you start?

 TRANSFER TO TEACHING

- ♦ Ask students to identify their Present State in terms of learning English. For their Desired State, ask them where they want to be – which may well realistically be far short of native-speaker level.
- ♦ This activity can also be done using three mime representations, or using sounds (groans, squeaks, laughter, songs, clapping, stamping, whatever).

Follow your dreams

A sixteen-year old American called Monty once had to write a composition about what he wanted to do when he grew up. He took a lot of trouble over it and spent hours writing about his dream of one day being the owner of a horse ranch. He wrote seven pages describing the 200-acre ranch in great detail, and drew a diagram showing the location of all the buildings, the stables and the track. He even drew a detailed floor plan of the 4,000 square-foot house that he would build. The next day he handed it in to his teacher.

Two days later his teacher handed it back. With a big, red F on the front. And the words: 'See me after class'.

After class, the boy with the dream asked his teacher why he had got an F, and the teacher said: 'Because this is an impossible dream for a boy like you. You need lots and lots of money to own a horse ranch. What sort of money have you got? Nothing. You come from a very poor family. There's no way you could ever do it. It's just not possible. I'll tell you what. You go back and write another composition with a more realistic goal, and I'll give you a different mark.'

The boy went home and asked his father for advice. His father said: 'I'm sorry I can't help you, but I think this has to be your decision, and I have a sense that it's going to be a really important one for you.' The boy thought about it for a week. Finally he handed back the same paper to his teacher, saying 'You can keep the F. I'll keep my dream.'

Monty then turned to the group of people with him and said: 'I tell you this story because you are all sitting in my 4,000 square-foot house in the middle of my 200-acre horse ranch. And that composition is framed over the fireplace.' He went on: 'The best part of the story is that two summers ago, that same teacher brought 30 kids to camp out on my ranch for a week. When he was leaving, he said: "Look Monty, I can tell you this now. When I was your teacher I was a bit of a dreamstealer. I'm sorry to say that I stole of lot of kids' dreams in those days. But I'm glad you had the courage to hang on to yours."

'Don't let anyone steal your dreams. No matter what, follow your heart.'

Criteria for well-formed outcomes

The way we express an outcome in words affects whether or not we achieve it. To make your outcomes more achievable, check them against the PEACH-S criteria. There are several variations of these criteria in NLP, but they are all very similar and they all serve the same purpose: to help you to make sure that your outcome is stated in a way that helps you to attain it.

"Great minds must be ready not only to take opportunities, but to make them."

COLTON

Write down an outcome you would like – big, small or medium-sized. You could perhaps put into words the outcome you used in 'Doodle a link'. Match your outcome against the PEACH-S criteria. Make notes and amendments as you go and at the end write your clearly-defined outcome.

PEACH-S CRITERIA

P = Positive

State your outcome in the affirmative rather than the negative. Think about what you do want rather than what you don't want, in order to be able to imagine it and begin to move towards it. You can only move away from something you don't want.

NO to negatives:
I don't want to be an air-traffic controller.

YES to affirmatives:
I want to be a teacher.

Be careful … some outcomes are negatives in disguise: *I want to stop smoking* and *I want to lose weight*, for example, are not positive in the same way as **I want to breathe easily and be fit and healthy** and **I want to attain my ideal shape.**

E = Evidence

How will you know that you've achieved your outcome? What will your test be? Can you imagine what it will be like? Do you have a clear representation of yourself? Can you see/hear/feel yourself having achieved it? What will other people notice about you that is different?

A = All the time?

Do you want this outcome all the time and everywhere? Or do you only want it at certain times and in certain places? If you want to be 'in control' at work, do you also want to be 'in control' at home? If your outcome is to be playful with your children, do you also want to be playful with your boss? You might, but just think it through and define clearly in what contexts and with whom you want the outcome.

C = Consequences

What are the consequences of the outcome? Form a clear image of yourself having achieved the outcome and then ask yourself the following key questions:
1   Is this outcome really me? Does it fit with my sense of who I am?
2   How does this outcome affect other people in my life? My family? My friends? My colleagues?
3   Is this really the outcome I want? What will I lose and what will I gain? Do the disadvantages outweigh the advantages?
4   Can I modify the outcome to make the first three answers more positive?

Some people at this stage realise that what they've been wishing for isn't what they want at all – which is a very useful thing to learn. It frees you up to think again about what you really do want, so you can start moving towards that.

H = Hands

Is this outcome in your hands? Is it under your control? 'I'm dreaming of a white Christmas' is not a well-formed outcome! Is the outcome for you or for someone else? Outcomes for other people tend not to work. 'I want my boss to be nicer' is not a well-formed outcome. You can't change your boss (although you can act in a way which makes it more likely that your boss will act more pleasantly to you).

S = Spirit

How does this outcome fit into your wider sense of where you're going in life? How does it connect with what your life is all about? Does it accord with the spirit of your life, or your sense of mission, if you have one?

 STEPPING UP AND
STEPPING DOWN

Stepping up

Having a sense of where an outcome is leading us and how it ties up with larger dreams and desires can confirm us in our belief that this is an appropriate outcome for us. It can also strengthen our resolve to reach that outcome.

"Be careful about what you want, you might get it"

Emerson

An important question to ask yourself about any outcome is:

If I had that outcome, what would it do for me?

And then ask another question based on the answer:

And if I had that other thing, what would that do for me?

And keep going up and up and up, using each answer as the basis for a new question, until you think you can go no further … and then go up a tiny bit more!

Stepping down

Whenever we have an outcome, some sort of obstacle is presupposed, otherwise we'd already be there. Stepping down is a way of uncovering what the obstacles might be, so we can begin to deal with them if we choose to. We may alternatively decide to modify our outcome or possibly even abandon it altogether.

Here is an unconcluded example:

O   *My outcome is to sing really well.*

Q   *So what stops me?*

A   *Partly time to go to singing lessons and practise, but mainly fear of failure.*

Q   *So what would I want instead of fear of failure?*

A   *Confidence, belief that I can do it.*

Q   *So what stops me believing I can do it?*

A   *A voice in my head telling me I can't!*

Q   *So what would I want instead of that voice in my head?*

You can step down, using two questions alternately:

Q1   *What stops me?*

Q2   *What would I want instead of the thing that stops me?*

"There is no right way to do the wrong thing."

You can use this strategy to help someone else to explore an outcome too, by changing *'me'* and *'I'* to *'you'*.

Do it now

- Choose an outcome that you have.
- Check that it's well-formed.
- Step it up, then step it down.
- Then step it up again – it's nice to finish on a high note!

Looking forward, looking around

We've stressed the importance of having outcomes. It's also important, however, not to focus so much on the future that we miss the present. Don't miss the look in your children's eyes today, because you're thinking about how to get them to the dentist tomorrow. It's important, too, not to be blinkered to what is around us, but rather to be aware of and open to possibilities as they arise. There will certainly be times in our life when we just want to 'go with the flow' and see what happens.

"Our aspirations are our possibilities."

ROBERT BROWNING

When you are moving towards an objective, it is very important to pay attention to the road. It is the road that teaches us the best way to get there, and the road enriches us as we walk its length. And it is the same thing when you have an objective in your life. It will turn out to be better or worse depending on the route you choose to reach it and the way you negotiate that route.

The Pilgrimage by Paulo Coelho

A good meal, like a poem or a life, has a certain balance and diversity, a certain coherence and fit. As one learns to cope in the kitchen, one no longer duplicates whole meals but rather manipulates components and the way they are put together.

The improvised meal will be different from the planned meal, and certainly riskier, but rich with the possibility of delicious surprise.

Improvisation can be either a last resort or an established way of evoking creativity.

Sometimes a pattern chosen by default can become a path of preference.

Composing a Life by Mary Catherine Bateson

'TOTE' for lesson planning

TOTE is an NLP model for putting outcomes into action.

Test	Check where you're up to
Operate	Try out a way of achieving your objective
Test	Check that you have achieved your objective
Exit	Stop – and move on to the next objective

The model is really **TO [TOTOTO...] TE.** Test/Operate as many times as necessary to achieve the objective before you Exit. We like to remind ourselves to set a clear outcome before we start, so our model is Outcome – **TO[TOTOTO...]TE.**

You might like to use the following version of the model for lesson planning.

- Set clear outcomes for your lessons in terms of content and what you want students to achieve. Take into account the physical surroundings and the physical, mental and emotional well-being of the students. Consider also how you're going to achieve the outcomes, what techniques you will use, how you can incorporate a variety of activities to accommodate different learning styles, etc.

- Follow the lesson plan. Be flexible and ready to make necessary changes according to the needs of your students at the time.

- Evaluate the lesson. Did the students achieve your outcomes? Did you notice them achieving any of their own? Did you achieve your own outcomes? Note any changes you made in the course of the lesson. Note any changes you could make to this lesson, or to your teaching in the future. Ask yourself: 'What could I have done differently to achieve a different result? How could this lesson be more elegant next time?'

- Operate/Test every time you teach the lesson (or any lesson).

- Exit? We haven't yet reached this stage. We look for improvement every time we teach anything – and carry our learning into the next lesson.

 WORDSTORM

Think back over this section on outcomes and write down any words which you think will help you to remember the key points. (See page 24)

Then turn your WORDSTORM into a WORDTRAIL. Sequence the words in a way which recaptures the flow of the ideas.

How language relates to experience

The **world,** our **experience** of the world and the **language** we use to describe our experience of the world are not the same thing. They are three different things.

When we experience the world as it is objectively, we filter it through our senses and neurological processes. Our experience, therefore, is at one remove from the world itself. We then put our experience and our interpretation of it into words. The language we use is at one remove from the experience. It is at two removes from the world itself. The language is different from the world and a distortion of it.

In order to put our experience into language – our meanings into words – we are necessarily imprecise. If we said exactly what we meant, we would have to choose our words very, very carefully and constantly check and double-check that what we understood was exactly what our listener understood. We would have to say everything about everything, leaving nothing out.

But we don't. If we did, it would take us all day to answer the greeting 'Hello. How are you?' Instead, we simplify and we use language economically. We assume that the other person uses and understands words in the same way we do and knows what we are talking about. And they do, more or less, most of the time. But in that 'more or less' there is room for misunderstanding each other ... and ourselves. These misunderstandings can sometimes lead to problems – or rather, challenges.

Basically we do three things:

We **distort,** for example by adding our emotions, values and beliefs: *'I saw a man behaving in an appalling way this morning. He was swearing at his dog!'* Do you think it is 'appalling' to swear? What about swearing at a dog? Define 'swearing'.

We **delete,** for example by assuming that other people know what or who we are talking about: *'Look at that. Isn't it great?'* What exactly are you talking about? Which precise bit of the scene is great? Define 'great'.

We **generalise,** eg by taking one example as representative of all of its kind. (This is a great starting point for racial and other forms of discrimination.) *'Men are better cooks.'* All men? Better than who?

In addition, people can simply speak very imprecisely. What do you think the writers of these sentences really meant to say when they wrote the following?*

- *This is to let you know that there is a smell coming from the man next door.*

- *My toilet is blocked and we can't bathe the children until it is cleared.*

- *Our kitchen floor is very damp, we have two children and would like a third, so will you send someone to do something about it?*

- *Will you please send someone to mend our broken path? Yesterday my wife tripped and fell on it and is now pregnant.*

If we want to be more precise, or help others to be more precise, we must look at how our linguistic assumptions can lead to imprecision in our communication and in our thinking. Then we can question the assumptions. We can improve communication with others by challenging the imprecise language we all use, both when we speak to others and when we speak to ourselves.

"There's nothing either good or bad, but thinking makes it so."
WILLIAM SHAKESPEARE

Challenging the language we use to ourselves can also help us to unblock our thinking. There isn't a problem first and then a way of thinking about it. The way of thinking *is* the problem. Changing our language can change our thinking ... and that gives us more choices about how to act.

The **Meta Model** is a tool inspired by Chomsky's Transformational Grammar and adapted by Bandler and Grinder** to challenge linguistic imprecision. It is a list of different distortions, deletions and generalisations (often called **Meta Model violations**) and a parallel list of suggestions for challenging them (**challenges**). The Meta Model is too large to be described here in its entirety, so we shall consider a sub-set of five Meta Model violations with their challenges, sometimes known as the **Precision Model.** (See next page)

The purpose of the challenges is to get speakers to be more precise, to express themselves more clearly, and in so doing hopefully to realise that what they've said is not actually true. But be careful not to undo people's positive beliefs. Take care only to challenge language which is limiting. The 'can't' in *'I can't hit the butcher on the head'*, for example, is not limiting like the 'can't' in *'I can't sing'*.

Why not cover the side of the page with the CHALLENGES to start with? Then as you read each example of a VIOLATION, imagine how you might challenge it. The challenges are written as though you are challenging someone else, but of course you can equally use them to challenge yourself!

---

* These are genuine extracts from letters received by a local council.
** In *The Structure of Magic* (See Booklist)

THE PRECISION MODEL

VIOLATIONS	CHALLENGES

Simple deletions (where crucial information is not given)

I don't understand.	What exactly don't you understand?
I'm hopeless.	At what? / In what way?
I'm depressed.	How exactly are you depressed?

Universal quantifiers (always, never, every-, no-, any-, all)

Nobody loves me.	Doesn't anyone love you?
	or Nobody? Not one person?
I'm always a mess.	Always? Hasn't there ever been an exception?
	or Yes, you're always a mess. Every single time I see you, without exception! (This is to goad the person into contradicting you.)

Comparative deletions (where the other half of the comparison is not specified)

I want to be a better teacher.	Better than what? Better in what way?
	or On a scale of 1 to 10, where are you now? How much better do you want to be?

Modal operators of necessity (must, need, ought to, should, have to)

I must get home to get dinner.	What makes that necessary?
	or What would happen if you didn't?

Modal operators of impossibility (can't, it's impossible …)

I can't relax.	What stops you relaxing?
	or Do you mean 'I can't' or do you mean 'I don't want to'?
It's impossible for me to go.	What would happen if you did?
	or What would you need in order to be able to relax?

You may have noticed that the question 'Why?' is rarely used as a challenge in this model. The reason is that 'Why?' questions tend not to lead to unpicking language and rethinking the issue. They tend rather to lead to justifying, denying, or expounding the beliefs that underlie the statement, while leaving the statement itself unchallenged … and unchanged.

Listen out for these violations both when other people say them and when you do, either out loud or to yourself. Challenge them when you hear them, and do it gently and 'rapportfully', not like an inquisition! (This is Meta Model, not Meta Murder!) Be curious, and find out what happens.

Challenges

What challenges can you think of for these statements?*

1 *I don't understand anything.*
2 *I ought to give up.*
3 *I can't do this exercise.*
4 *I never remember irregular verbs.*
5 *I want more grammar.*

6 *I mustn't let you down.*
7 *I'm not making any progress.*
8 *I don't know.*
9 *I want to improve my pronunciation.*
10 *It's impossible for me to learn English!*

TRANSFER TO TEACHING

Watch those modals and other deceptively dangerous words. Notice how you use them. Listen to how your students use them. And think about how you teach them too. We find the **Precision Model** adds a fascinating dimension to our teaching as we explore with students what people say, what people think they mean and what they actually mean. Modals can be fun!

In her book 'Making Contact', Virginia Satir wrote this:

What makes it possible to enhance our feelings of self-esteem is our willingness to be open to new possibilities, to try them on for size, and then, if they fit us, to practise using them until they are ours.

To start the process I have developed something I have called 'The Five Freedoms' –

- *The freedom to see and hear what is here instead of what should be, was or will be.*

- *The freedom to say what one feels and thinks, instead of what one should.*

- *The freedom to feel what one feels, instead of what one ought.*

- *The freedom to ask for what one wants, instead of always waiting for permission.*

- *The freedom to take risks in one's own behalf, instead of choosing to be only 'secure' and not rocking the boat.*

SUGGESTED ANSWERS

---

* 1 What, nothing? Not one thing? or Tell me something that you do understand. 2 What makes that necessary? or Who says? 3 What stops you? What do you need in order to do it? 4 Never? Haven't you ever remembered just one irregular verb? (+ How did you do so?) 5 How much more grammar do you want? 6 What would happen if you did? 7 None at all? Are you exactly where you were this time last year? 8 What exactly don't you know? or If you did know, what would you know? 9 In what way? By how much? 10 So you've learned absolutely nothing up to now? (or if student has spoken in English) Well you've learned to say that!

Guided fantasy: Your garden

Take a deep breath and close your eyes and imagine for a moment the most wonderful garden. And now imagine yourself as the person responsible for that garden. You are the gardener. Be in your garden.

Look around your lovely garden for a moment and just see all the magnificent things growing there. Perhaps there are flowers. Perhaps there are fruit trees. Perhaps there are wonderful vegetables. You choose what is growing in your garden. You can grow whatever you like.

You can also have statues, arches, ponds, fountains … whatever you want.

As you walk around your garden, see all the colours in your mind's eye. Smell the gorgeous smells. Hear the sound of the birds and insects. Feel the sensation of your feet on the ground as you walk. Feel the air against your face. Feel too a sense of pride in everything that you can see around you. Really enjoy your garden. Really enjoy everything that you can see and hear and smell and feel.

And as you walk around your garden, be aware too of all the things that are not yet visible. Things you planted a while ago but which have not yet come up. Seeds or bulbs which will one day emerge and flower and flourish. Just imagine how it will be when that happens and how your garden will be even more beautiful as a result. And be glad.

And be aware too as you walk that though plants wither and die, other plants will come to take their place. Plants that will grow and blossom and smell heavenly. And the cycle will go on. And you are a part of that. You help it to happen.

Take a moment just to plant a few more seeds. There is a patch of newly dug earth, so all you need to do is scatter the seeds on the ground and then place some earth over them. There's a watering can nearby. Pick it up and sprinkle water over the earth.

And then look round your garden again and notice a special tree, plant or flower. Go up to it and look at it closely. Smell it. How does it smell? Touch it gently. How does it feel to touch? Just take a moment to really appreciate it. And be very glad that it's there. That it's part of your garden.

In this special place you can find the answer to anything you need to know. Ask the question: 'What is it I most need to know right now?' Wait a moment for the answer and trust that it will be there whether you know it consciously or not.

Look around your garden once more and feel again that sense of joy. Prepare to leave your garden, knowing that you can come back whenever you choose. Take a deep breath and slowly and gently, come back to the room, bringing with you that sense of gladness and joy, and taking it with you into the rest of your day.

The resources we need are within us

Resources in NLP are positive qualities such as a sense of humour, confidence, patience, good listening skills, and so on. We have the resources we need to make the changes we want to.

The problem is that, although we may have a particular resource in certain contexts in our life, we may not have it in another context where we need it. For example, Jane has learnt to be quite brave when it comes to getting into freezing cold water for a winter dip, but she has always been a bit pathetic about going to the dentist. So she has learned to transfer the 'cold-water' strategy to the dentist's waiting room so she has the courage to boldly go into the surgery when the moment arrives.

"In the midst of winter
I finally learned
That there was in me
An invincible summer."

ALBERT CAMUS

It's important to make a distinction between 'resources' and 'skills'. We don't necessarily have the practical skills to fly a Boeing 747, for example. What we do have, however, is the ability to learn. If something is humanly possible in the world, then it's possible for us to do it too, but we obviously have to learn the practical skills needed and practise them until we can do it.

But do it we can.

This section concentrates on helping you become aware of your resources. The section on anchoring (on page 83) will show you how to transfer a resource from one area of your life where you have it, to another where you need it.

:::::::::::::::::::::::::::::::::::: **Implications** ::::::::::::::::::::::::::::::::::::

- ◆ It's very easy to be aware of our weaknesses. Be aware of your strengths too for a change.

- ◆ Help students to be aware of what they're good at – whatever it is, and however irrelevant it might seem to what they're learning (for it never is).

- ◆ Help them to analyse how they're good at things, so they can use the same strategies in other contexts where they think they're not so good.

- ◆ You can transfer resources you have in one area of your life to another area where you don't.

'Tis too high
Come to the edge
We might fall
Come to the edge
So they came to the edge
And he pushed them
And they flew

APOLLINAIRE

LIFELINE

Draw a line and mark against it the key events in your life. Focus particularly on events which illustrate an aspect of your character, where you learnt something significant, or where you gained a skill or resource (sense of humour, courage, humility, etc).

When you have finished, review your lifeline in relation to the following questions.

1 What were the turning points?

2 What patterns of experience, achievement or lessons can you see?

3 Which things enhanced and enriched your life?

4 Which things would you avoid in future?

5 What were the positive outcomes or intentions of any negative events?

6 What does the purpose of your life seem to have been so far?

7 What resources have you gained? Link specific resources to specific moments or events.

8 What have you learnt … from life? … from doing this activity?

TRANSFER TO TEACHING

Students enjoy this activity as a very personal way of practising the past simple. The lifelines can be drawn and illustrated to go on the wall. Students have the option of putting symbols for significant events they don't want to share publicly. The notes can be used as the starting point for a short written autobiography. You could introduce the activity by exploring the key moments in the lifeline example which is given here.

62	born
65	loved primary school – and teacher
67	brother David born – jealous
68	parents divorced – blamed David Lived with aunt
70	Mum remarried – went home; didn't belong
73	boarding school – read a lot; guitar lessons
78/79	wonderful French holidays with Sarah Passed exams – just!
81	back-packing in Asia – gained courage and independence
82	university – lots of boyfriends
85	year in France – country wonderful, teaching terrible
86	language degree – phew! Temp. clerical jobs
88	creative writing classes
89	took up yoga and meditation
90	EFL qualification – I'm a brill teacher Teaching in France
92	Married Claude
95	'Changes' published – I'm an author!
97	Jacqueline born – I'm a mother!
	wife?
	mother?
	teacher?
	writer?
	?
	travel

JOB APPLICATION

1 Make a list of all the roles you play in life, eg business partner, mother, lover, neighbour, counsellor (for friends' problems), plumber, cleaner, artist, mathematician (children's homework, supermarket checkout), cook, etc. One role per line.

2 Imagine each of your roles is a job you are applying for. Alongside each one, write down the personal qualities you bring to each job. Remember you really, really need this job, so only write down the qualities which will help you to get it. (You have to be honest, although a little exaggeration is only to be expected.)

"Nothing we ever imagined is beyond our powers, only beyond our present self-knowledge."

THEODORE ROSZAK

3 Talented, aren't you? If you have any other qualities you don't seem to be using at the moment, write them down now.

4 When you've finished, look at the 'jobs' for which you don't seem to have a lot of qualities and see whether you could add any of the qualities that you have in other areas.

Finding resources

At various times in our NLP training we've been asked to 'go inside and think of a time when you were happy (or confident, or had the quality you need now, or whatever)'. Put on the spot like that, our minds came up blank. Often the problem was finding a 'pure' memory, a moment that wasn't 'contaminated' with what came before or after it. Sometimes the problem was finding any relevant memory at all.

Then we discovered that at some point we'd both sat down and consciously thought back through our lives to come up with a store of relevant memories. We recommend that you do the same. Think of happy times or successful times or funny incidents or moments of joy. It only needs to be a moment and it doesn't have to be something huge. A special dawn or sunset, the moment when you realised you were riding a bike alone, being generous to someone, a particular song or piece of music, the smell of a certain flower – whatever brings back that warm glow for you.

We've included several tasks in this book to encourage the conscious recall of memories. We also think that they will be particularly helpful for anyone whose first language is not English, so that they can sort out useful language while a dictionary is to hand! Once you start looking, your non-conscious mind carries on the search. It's amazing the number of wonderful memories that come flooding back when you aren't even thinking about it. Write them all down. Enjoy them.

Incidentally, when we can't think of a relevant memory, we fake it. We imagine how such a memory would have been. And it works. And other times, when we stop panicking and just get on with the activity, our non-conscious mind comes up with something right on cue.

Don't just read the book. Do the activities. You may find they work for you too.

The Ugly Duckling

nce upon a summertime a mother duck sat upon her eggs. At noon one day, when the sun was high in the sky, one by one the eggs began to crack and the little ducklings emerged. 'Peep, peep!' said each little ducking as it came out. 'Quack, quack!' replied the mother duck.

All the eggs had cracked except one, the largest one. And so the mother duck continued to sit on it. The great egg broke open at last. 'Peep, peep!' said the little one as it came out. Except it wasn't so little! How large and ugly it was! 'Perhaps it's a turkey,' thought the mother duck.

The next day the mother duck took the ducklings swimming. The ugly grey one swam about with the others. 'No, it's not a turkey,' thought the mother duck. Afterwards they walked through a farmyard. The other ducks in the yard looked at them and shouted, 'How ugly that one is! We won't have it!' And they flew at the ugly duckling and bit him on the neck. 'Leave him alone,' said his mother, 'he's not doing you any harm.' But they kept biting him until the little duck family left the farmyard.

And so it continued. Day after day, the poor ugly duckling was bitten and pecked and teased by all the other ducks. And the hens. And the turkeys too. Even his brothers and sisters were unkind to him. And so one day, he ran away. He ran through the hedge and over the moor. And every animal he met was rude or unkind to him. Until one morning he awoke, terrified, to find a hunting dog with huge sharp teeth sniffing him. But the dog just turned away and bounded off. 'I'm so ugly, even the dog doesn't want to bite me,' said the ugly duckling. And he was very sad and very, very lonely. And the autumn came, and the leaves turned yellow and brown and it began to get cold.

One evening, just as the sun was setting, he saw a flock of large white birds flying overhead. They were swans, but the ugly duckling didn't know that then. He just thought how incredibly beautiful they were, and he loved them as he had never loved anything in his life.

And the winter came and oh! the ugly duckling was so miserable, and oh! he suffered so much. One night it was so cold that the water froze around his legs and he was trapped. He looked up at the stars and resigned himself to death. But somehow he survived.

And then it was spring once more. And early one morning, the ugly duckling came across three swans on a lake. 'I don't want to suffer any more,' he thought, 'I'd rather be killed by these noble creatures.' And he swam towards them and bowed his head. But what did he see in the water? Not a plump, ugly, grey bird, but a graceful white bird! The three swans swam round him. 'Welcome!' they cried, and they stroked his neck with their beaks.

And some children on the edge of the lake shouted: 'Look, there's a new swan! And it's the most beautiful of all.'

The beautiful swan felt that his heart would burst with thankfulness and love.

Submodalities: exploring your imagination

Remember 'Meet your mind', the task you did back on page 24? Well, just as the pictures in your mind's eye can be different from other people's, so can internal sounds and feelings. You'll probably also find differences in your own images depending on what you are thinking about. Internal representational systems can also be called 'modalities'. Their differences and characteristics (sub-categories) are known as **submodalities.** Since many of the NLP techniques for making changes (the 'programming' part of NLP) involve manipulating your internal rep systems, you might like to keep a record of how your imagination works.

On the next two pages, we list many of the common variations in the VAK submodalities, although not all of them will be relevant to everyone or to every experience. Most people can answer the questions about visualising, even if they don't see clear pictures. The differences in Auditory and Kinaesthetic imagination are not always so clear cut, so we have given suggestions and invite you to refer to them or add your own distinctions. Olfactory and Gustatory distinctions are not so well documented, so make notes about anything you notice.

POSITIVE/NEGATIVE

Think of any recent situation or event which you experienced as positive. Recreate the scene as fully as possible. See what you saw at the time. Hear what you heard. Feel what you felt.

Read through the list of submodalities and questions on the next pages. Answer as many questions as you can in relation to the re-creation of your positive event.

You may find some questions very easy to answer, and others less so. You may find that questions in one submodality are easier for you to answer than questions in others. Don't struggle for hours trying to access the timbre of your uncle Bert's voice. Just notice what's easy for you and what isn't. It's all useful information. And when you come to play with your submodalities, it makes sense to manipulate those that you're most aware of.

Now explore the differences between your submodalities for a positive experience and those for a negative one. Recreate in your mind something which did not go as well as you wanted it to. (Please choose a reasonably minor negative experience, such as a setback at work, rather than a major catastrophe.) Explore the submodalities in the same way as you did for the positive experience. Is one brighter, or bigger than the other? Is it in a different place? Closer or further away? Louder or softer?

Make a particular note of differences between the two experiences which are significant in terms of submodalities.

Finish off by immersing yourself in the positive experience again.

You could also examine the differences between past and future, things you are sure or unsure about, people you like and people you don't like, and so on.

VISUAL SUBMODALITIES

Location	Where is your picture? Point to it. Is it ... up? down? in front? behind?	_____
Distance	How close or far away is it?	_____
Size	How big or small is it?	_____
Colour	Is it in colour or black and white?	_____
Movement	Is it moving (like a film or video) or still (like a photo)?	_____
Dimension	2D? 3D?	_____
Brightness	How bright or dull is it?	_____
Definition	How clear or hazy is it?	_____
Shape	Is it square? rectangular? triangular? round? indefinite? pear-shaped? (Anything is possible!)	_____
Association*	Can you see yourself in the picture or are you looking through your own eyes?	_____
Edging	Does the picture have a frame or does it merge into its surroundings?	_____
Quantity	Is there just one picture or are there two or more?	_____
Other	What else have you noticed?	_____
		_____
		_____

AUDITORY SUBMODALITIES

Nature	Are there sounds or a voice or voices? Or a mix?	_____
Quantity	Is there one voice or sound, or are there more?	_____
Location	Where are the voices and/or sounds coming from?	_____
Mono/stereo	More in one ear than another?	_____
Distance	How close or far away are they?	_____
Volume	How loud or quiet?	_____
Tempo/speed	How fast or slow?	_____
Rhythm	Gentle, punchy .... what?	_____
Tonality	Is there a variety of tones or a monotone?	_____
Timbre	Tinny? Mellow? Screeching? What?	_____
Duration	How long does it go on for?	_____
Quality	How clear or distorted/muffled? Echo? Reverberation?	_____
Pitch	How high or low?	_____
Ownership	Your voice or someone else's?	_____
Other	What else have you noticed?	_____
		_____
		_____

---

* **association** means being inside the experience; **dissociation** means watching the experience from outside

KINAESTHETIC SUBMODALITIES

Quantity	Is there just one feeling or more than one?	_____
Location	Where is the feeling?	_____
Size	How big or small is it?	_____
Shape	Is it a definite or indefinite shape? If definite, what shape is it?	_____
Temperature	How hot, warm, cool or cold?	_____
Colour	Does it have a particular colour?	_____
Intensity	How strong or slight?	_____
Movement	Does it move around or is it still?	_____
Direction	If it moves, which way does it go?	_____
Growth	Does it increase or decrease in size or stay the same?	_____
Duration	How short or long-lived is it?	_____
Constancy	Is it there all the time, or is it intermittent?	_____
Rhythm	Does it pulsate with a particular beat?	_____
Breath	Does it affect your breathing in any way?	_____
Tactile	Can you touch it or feel it with any part of your body? Is it rough, smooth, realistic?	_____
Other	What else have you noticed?	_____
		_____
		_____

OLFACTORY / GUSTATORY SUBMODALITIES

Any characteristics you notice

_____

_____

_____

Analogue and digital submodalities

Differentiating between **analogue** and **digital** submodalities can be helpful because it can affect how we make changes in the way we represent things to ourselves.

Analogue submodalities are those which are on a sliding scale. They can be increased or decreased in some way. Examples are temperature, volume or size.

Digital submodalities are those which are either one thing or the other, and tend to come in pairs of opposites. You can switch them on or off. Examples are association/dissociation, mono/stereo and movement/stasis.

How many digital submodalities can you identify in the list? (Clue: They're the ones where you can't ask the question 'How + adjective'.)*

──────────── SUGGESTED ANSWERS ────────────

* location, colour (v black + white), shape, association, edging, quantity, nature, ownership, movement, direction, constancy

PLAY WITH YOUR SUBMODALITIES

Think of a time when you felt very positive and resourceful. Whether you have a picture, sounds or feelings, or a mixture, notice the submodalities involved. Take your time to establish a clear memory.

Play with your submodalities! Ask yourself 'What happens if …..?' What happens if I make the picture brighter? Is it different if I make it darker? What about bigger or smaller? Higher or lower? Black and white or colour? How do the changes affect how you feel about the memory? Can you make it better, more enjoyable, more intense? Remember that you can always put things back as they were. Look at the scene from the outside (dissociated), then step in and fully associate into the experience. This usually makes a significant difference.

Play with the sound too. And tactile feelings. Can you smell or taste anything? Can you make changes to smells and tastes? How about emotions? Can you make them stronger or weaker? Move the feeling to different parts of your body – to your shoulder – your elbow – your thumb. See the feeling as a colour. Change the colour.

If you're having problems, try putting your mental image on a TV screen. Adjust the brightness knob or the volume. There are knobs to make other changes too. Or you can change the camera angle, have split screen, have still or moving pictures, run the sequence backwards and forwards, faster and slower, and so on.

If you still can't do something, try doing the opposite. If you can make something smaller but not bigger, make it smaller; then reverse the process to take it back to the original size … and then continue what you're now doing, making it bigger!

The only limitations are ones you have put on yourself. If you can't do something, just say 'Yes I can'. Imagine how it would be if you could do it, and then do it!

The more changes you can make, the more control you will have over your imaging. Your imagination is the limit. Have fun. Play. And notice the effect.

Now go back to the original memory. Add the changes that make it better. Move it backwards and forwards until it's exactly the right distance away. Make it bigger or smaller until it's exactly the right size. Try wrapping it around you. Get right inside it. Turn up the colours and the volume … till it's perfect. Make any changes you want … and then double the feeling. And double it again. And really enjoy it.

TRANSFER TO TEACHING

Students enjoy playing with their submodalities. There is obvious scope for practising comparatives, they practise a large amount of vocabulary and are very keen to find ways to express themselves. Follow the instructions much as we've given them here for you, asking them to work in pairs or small groups.

Associating / dissociating

If you have to discipline students, try to dissociate first. Put yourself in the role of a person who is disciplining. Keep the situation impersonal (for them as well as for you). Explain what is wrong and what needs to be done better. Then re-associate back to your generous giving self – uncontaminated by the negativity.

Imagineering

Once you know how your mind works and how you can work your mind, you can really start to have fun. Take up the new sport of 'imagineering' – modify your images until you've got them how you want them.

Have you got a memory which makes you feel bad? You've learnt your lesson, but you still feel bad? Do you have an irrational fear of something? Spiders? Flying? You know logically that there's nothing to be frightened of, but you're not going to let something as silly as logic stop you? Do you have a 'bad habit' that you want to break? Biting your nails? Something worse? Do you want to change? (If you don't want to change, go on to the next chapter). Try any or all of the following:

- Dissociate from a bad memory. Step outside and look at it. Make the picture smaller. Move it further away. Turn down the colours till it's black and white. Make it into a photograph which you can screw up and throw away. Or put it on a film screen with you in the cinema watching. Get further away still by moving back to the projection room and watching you watching the film. Make it into a cartoon. Make something incongruous happen. Run the film backwards. Run it at double speed – and half speed. Make people speak in high-pitched squeaky voices. Throw a bucket of water over everything.

- Associate into good memories and resourceful moments. Really be there. Make adjustments until you've highlighted the exact moment of greatest pleasure or achievement and work with that. Make it bigger, brighter, louder, more intense. Double the feeling and then double it again. Notice where the feeling comes from and where it goes to. Just before it stops, loop it round and start it again … and again … and again. Double it each time. Smile. Spread the feeling right round your body. Really enjoy it. How much pleasure can you stand?

- Try changing bad into good. Identify the bad memory or unwanted habit. and make it into a picture which you minimise in one of the ways above. Then identify a good memory or a picture of the result you want instead. Enhance it every way you can. Switch from one to the other several times, making the negative smaller and more insignificant each time and enhancing the positive. Switch quickly backwards and forwards from one to the other. Quicker! End with the positive and really enjoy it. Always end with the positive.

People are different. Even though there do seem to be some core submodalities which have more impact than others, the submodality changes that work most effectively for you will not necessarily work for other people. If you're working with someone else, find out the things that make a difference for them and use those.

When you have learnt to play down bad memories and enhance good ones, you will find it extremely useful to be able to 'anchor' the new and improved versions. Anchoring is the next Core Concept we look at (see page 83) and you may well wish to return here and 'imagineer' some more once you have read it.

Life levels: line up your life

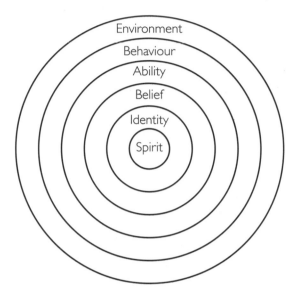

Our experience occurs at different levels, each affecting and being affected by the others. The **life levels** model is a useful way of exploring and integrating the different levels. Think about each one in relation to your own life.

1 Environment Ask: Where? (and When?)

Most of us live our lives in many different environments: at home, in the classroom or training-room, in the staffroom, at the gym, at social events …

2 Behaviour Ask: What?

In different environments, we do different things: at home we cook, we read, we watch television, we wash up …, in the classroom we teach …, in the staffroom we share ideas, we relax … and so on.

3 Ability Ask: How?

How do we do the things we do? What skills do we have that enable us to do the many and varied activities that we do in our life?

4 Belief Ask: Why?

Why are we able to do the things we do? What beliefs do we have that enable us to have those particular skills and that support us in what we do?

5 Identity Ask: Who am I?

What is my sense of myself. Who is this person who holds certain beliefs? Who is the core self at the root of all the many selves or roles that I play in my life? What is my essence?

"Know thyself."
PLATO

6 Spirit Ask: What else?

What is my life about? What does it mean? Why am I here? Where am I going? What do I want ultimately? *Those* sorts of questions.

Fulfilment comes from having all the levels in alignment. So, for example, if I am in a place I like, doing things I enjoy, using skills I am good at, sustained by positive and empowering beliefs, having a strong sense of all this being part of who I am and connected to a higher sense of purpose ... then that is wonderful. I am centred, connected, congruent and content.

On the other hand, having a level (or more) out of alignment, can lead to a sense of unease or even great unhappiness. If you have to behave in certain situations in ways which you feel are not 'you' or which compromise your beliefs, you are likely to be unhappy. If you are doing lots of things you enjoy at a superficial level, but which are ultimately leading you away from what you perceive as your ultimate goal in life, you may come to regret having 'wasted your time'.

Jane has certain beliefs about bringing up children and a certain sense of her identity as a mother, but she has on occasion shouted at her kids. In this instance, 'behaviour' is out of line with 'identity', 'belief' and also with 'ability'. The result is a feeling of incongruency ... and guilt!

So what can the life levels model do?

One thing it can help with is pinpointing where you need to focus your attention and perhaps even make changes in your life. Another thing it can do is help you line everything up so you can be centred, connected and congruent. Another way in which we have found it very useful indeed is in exploring an outcome – see the activity below.

Dilts' model has sometimes been criticised for not being systematic and rigorous enough, and yet many people have used it to very beneficial effect. It is only a model. The questions you need to ask yourself are: 'Does it work for me?', 'Does it help me'. If you can answer 'yes', then use it.

:: **Implications** ::

Effective learning is a multi-level process. As a teacher, you need to ensure that all the levels are working to support the learning of your students. Make sure ...

- that the **environment** is as conducive as possible to learning and that adequate time is allocated for key activities

- that classroom **behaviour** and activities are relevant, interesting and useful

- that learners develop **abilities** and skills, and that they learn how to learn

- that learners **believe** that they can learn, and that they develop confidence

- that learners have a sense of themselves as proficient learners and users of language at the level of **identity**

- that learners have a sense of **spirit,** of their learning being worthwhile in a much wider sense

---

* The Life Level model was developed originally by Robert Dilts, drawing on the work of Gregory Bateson. It has also been called neurological levels, logical levels and nested levels of experience.

Preparation for Life Level Alignment

1 Write the name of each level on a separate piece of paper and place them in a line on the floor, leaving some space between each one:

ENVIRONMENT   BEHAVIOUR   ABILITY   BELIEF   IDENTITY   SPIRIT*

2 Think of an outcome you have or a particular situation or context you wish to explore. Or you can do this activity in an all-encompassing way with your life in general. Why not start with your teaching? You in the classroom.

3 You are going to step into each level, starting with the **environment** you are exploring. Every time you step into a different level, don't think about it in a detached, dissociated way. Really experience what it's like and **associate** into it. (See Submodalities page 74) Pick a specific moment and see it, hear it and feel it. When you have really associated into the experience, step out to the side of the line, before stepping into the next one.

"Here is a test to find whether your mission on earth is finished: If you're alive, it isn't."

RICHARD BACH

You are going to step into and out of all the levels in this way. Take as long as you like inside each level, and take thinking time between each if you wish. The value comes from taking time to really *experience* at each level.

We suggest you take one environment for your first experience, but it is also possible to get a sense of several environments at the same time, or choose one as representative. If it's a future environment, then just imagine it.

4 Before you begin, first read through **all** the steps for the procedure on page 81, so you know what you're going to be doing. It doesn't matter if you don't follow the steps exactly... so once you've got the general idea of the alignment, you may prefer to put aside the procedure and just do it. (The papers on the floor will help remind you). Alternatively, do the activity with a friend. Take turns and talk each other through the levels.

"To learn something effectively, learners need to know what to do. They need to know how to do it. They need to know why it is important. They need to know how it relates to who they are – their role. ... It's the sequencing and the mix of these levels that is the essence of instructional methodology and communication strategies."

ROBERT DILTS

---

* We use the word spirit rather than the often-used spirituality or mission, to avoid the religious and/or organisational connotations of those words, which some people find it difficult to relate to. Spirit can be religious, but it doesn't have to be. If you don't like the word spirit, change it to something you do like and which works for you. Change any of the other words too.

 LIFE LEVEL
ALIGNMENT

Have in mind a question or **outcome** for this activity and think of the environment you are going to explore.

1 Form a clear representation of the **environment** and when you're ready, step in and be there. Really experience the place. See it, hear it and feel it. And when you're ready, step out.

2 Think about your **behaviour** in the environment, either what you are doing now or what you are going to be doing. When you're ready, step into the second level and really experience yourself doing what you do. Step out.

3 Think about your **abilities.** Experience or re-experience the skills and resources you have that enable you to do the things that you do. You can also add other skills you use in different situations if you wish. When you're ready, step in and really experience fully a sense of these abilities. Step out.

4 In the fourth level, **belief,** access those beliefs that support and sustain you – whether you consciously used them in the previous levels or not. Step in. And when you're ready, step out.

5 In the fifth level, **identity,** be who you are. Have a sense of the fundamental you, and also of appropriate roles for your outcome or situation. You may well find that you are not in any particular place or role for this level. Step in. And when you're ready, step out.

6 When you step into the sixth level, **spirit,** take the time to really experience that special place and feel energised by it. If you have no definite sense of what it is, be assured that there is something there and just imagine how it would feel. In other words … go for it! Fake it if you have to – it works just as well! (We know!)

   Stay there! Don't step out.

   This is the key part. From your position in **spirit,** turn round and look back down the levels. You're going to step back down into the different levels, taking with you all the experience from this and each subsequent level. You'll probably want to move quite quickly back down the levels without the need to stop in between.

5 When you're ready, step back into **identity,** taking with you your sense of spirit. Re-experience who you are, this time enriched with your spirit.

4 Step into **belief,** taking with you your sense of spirit and identity. Re-access those beliefs once more, this time strengthened by your spirit and your identity.

3 Step into **ability,** taking everything else with you. Re-experience those skills and resources once more, supported by your spirit, identity and belief.

2 Step into **behaviour.** Experience doing those things once more, this time having with you your spirit, identity, belief and abilities.

1 When you're ready, step into **environment,** taking everything else with you. Be in that place once again, this time connected to your spirit, identity, belief, abilities and behaviour. (A bit like 'This is the house that Jack built'!)

   When you're ready, step out. How was it?

Intercultural awareness

As language teachers, we necessarily have to take into account intercultural differences. Language reflects the way people think. There are certain underlying cultural beliefs and values which express themselves in the way people behave – and speak. This is a context in which it is worth considering life levels, particularly environment, behaviour and belief.

When we look at the behaviour of other nationalities, it often seems bizarre or unreasonable. The British view of Italians, for example, is often that they are pushy or rude. They don't wait their turn in a queue. This offends British 'beliefs' in 'fair play' and 'politeness'. However, Italians usually don't mind if people get something before them. They also seem to be much more generous in giving to others than the British, who tend to keep a careful score of whose turn it is to give and how much. So it could be argued that the British tend to place far too much emphasis on 'superficial' politeness.

These are gross generalisations, but they are the basis of stereotyping and prejudice.

A worthwhile exercise is to look – ideally on video – at behaviour from the target culture which seems 'odd' or 'wrong'.

- Start from the assumption that 80% of what you see has a rational explanation in any culture.

- Watch the sequence of behaviour and write down precisely and objectively (without pre-judgement) what you see people actually doing.

- Write down what you think their underlying beliefs and values might be.

- Write down the underlying beliefs and values in your culture which you think are being ignored or violated.

- Then look at the sequence of behaviour again (possibly from a longer excerpt) and identify things people do which satisfy your own culture's beliefs in a different way.

Anchoring: recapturing good moments

One day in winter, on my return home, my mother, seeing that I was cold, offered me some tea, a thing I did not ordinarily take. I declined at first, and then, for no particular reason, changed my mind. She sent for one of those squat, plump little cakes called 'petites madeleines', which look as though they had been moulded in the fluted valve of a scallop shell. And soon, mechanically, dispirited after a dreary day with the prospect of a depressing morrow, I raised to my lips a spoonful of the tea in which I had soaked a morsel of the cake. No sooner had the warm liquid mixed with the crumbs touched my palate than a shiver ran through me and I stopped, intent upon the extraordinary thing that was happening to me. An exquisite pleasure had invaded my senses, something isolated, detached, with no suggestion of its origin. And at once the vicissitudes of life had become indifferent to me, its disasters innocuous, its brevity illusory – this new sensation having had the effect, which love has, of filling me with a precious essence; or rather this essence was not in me, it was me. I had ceased to feel mediocre, contingent, mortal. Whence could it have come to me, this all-powerful joy? I sensed that it was connected with the taste of the tea and the cake, but that it infinitely transcended those savours, could not, indeed, be of the same nature. Where did it come from? What did it mean? How could I seize and apprehend it?

Marcel Proust – In Search of Lost Time

When Susan and Jane did the firewalk, we were told to do certain things to help us walk across a bed of hot coals. Before we began to walk, we looked up, so as to access *visually* and not *kinaesthetically*, and we visualised ourselves safely at the end of the walk. We breathed shallowly, and as we walked we said to ourselves: 'Cool moss, cool moss …' At the end of the walk, we brushed our feet (to get rid of any hot coals between our toes) and then made a clenched fist.

Why did we have to clench our fists?

Imagine the sort of state we were in having just done the firewalk. We were glowing with achievement. We'd just done something we hadn't really believed possible and we felt we could do almost anything. We felt incredibly powerful and confident. Clenching your fist 'anchors' it. It means that you can bring back that powerful, confident state any time you want to, just by clenching your fist.

The more you add powerful experiences to that fist in the meantime, the stronger your anchor becomes. So if you clench your fist again, every time you feel happy or do something that makes you feel very positive about yourself, that anchor becomes stronger and stronger … ready to be fired whenever you need it!

A bonus is that you become aware of how many times you do feel positive in a day that you might otherwise have missed!

Remember Ivan Pavlov and his dogs? Every time Pavlov fed his dogs, he rang a bell. The dogs salivated when they saw and smelt their food. After being fed several times accompanied by the sound of a bell, the dogs began to salivate as soon as they heard the bell, even when they didn't receive any food. The dogs had made an association between the bell and food. The bell became an anchor which triggered their response to food, salivation.

In humans, anchoring happens, for example, when we hear a song and it reminds us of a particular person, or a certain taste takes us back to a special place with all its associated feelings. The song and the taste are anchors for the experience. They are associated with the person or the place, and when we hear them or taste them again they 'trigger' the memory, as the tea and the cake did for Proust.

Like many things in NLP, anchoring is a way of making conscious and deliberate something that happens naturally. Anchoring is a way of making a deliberate connection between a state of mind and an 'anchor' (an action, a sound, a picture, etc), so that we can recall the state of mind simply by triggering the anchor. It is a way of making our resources available to us when we need them.

ACCESSING AND ANCHORING A USEFUL RESOURCE

We assume that you have worked through resources (pages 69-71) and submodalities (pages 73-77) before doing this activity.

READ THROUGH ALL THE INSTRUCTIONS BEFORE YOU BEGIN.

1 Choose your anchor. It must be something *quite specific* you can do discreetly in public and which you can *replicate exactly*. Try pressing your thumb against your first two fingers, or against your little finger, or squeezing your earlobe.

2 Think of a context (like speaking in front of a group of people, taking your driving test, going to an interview, etc) where you could use extra resources.

3 Think of a resource that would be useful in that context, such as confidence, a sense of humour, courage, determination, clear-thinking, quick-thinking, sensitivity, open-mindedness, etc.

4 Think of a time – in any context – when you experienced that quality, that particular state of mind. Choose an experience that is as 'purely positive' as possible, rather than one which is part good, part bad. Make sure you pinpoint the exact moment when you felt best.

5 Then relive that experience. Close your eyes. 'Go inside'. See what you saw then. Hear what you heard. Feel what you felt. Make sure you're 'associated', right inside the experience. Make it bigger, brighter, turn up the volume. Smile. Increase all the submodalities which make the experience more intense for you.

6 Do 5 again, and when the resourceful experience is at its peak, place your anchor, keeping it on for several seconds. Take it off just before the experience begins to subside. Do it again. Get into the experience. Turn up all the submodalities. Double the feeling. And anchor it. One more time. Get into it. Double the feelings. Bigger, brighter. Be in it. And anchor it.

7 Relax. Let go of the experience. Think about something else for a moment to change your state: what you had for breakfast, for example.

8 Test! Fire your anchor. Does it bring back the resourceful experience? Do you get a sense of having the resource you need? If you don't, go back and do steps 4 to 7 again, making sure that you follow the instructions exactly.

9 Finally, go back to step 2 and imagine yourself in the context which you found challenging. When you are really into it, fire your anchor. Notice the difference.

Go for it!

You needn't stop at anchoring one quality. You can repeat the activity with other helpful resources and anchor them all to the same spot. You keep adding ingredients until you have the right quantities. The only limit is the one you set.

Anchors can work in any rep system. Do you remember when your parent said your full name in *that* tone of voice. Yes, that one! Remember the feelings attached to it! Pavlov's dogs responded to an auditory anchor*.

Visual anchors work too. Facial expressions are particularly strong. And again close relatives seem to use them, with particular effect. *'Mummy, she's looking at me again!'*

Explore anchoring things in different rep systems and find out which is best for you. Watch out for anchors which occur naturally. Enjoy the positive ones and try to break the negative ones. Remember to consciously anchor the naturally-occurring good moments when they happen.

You can anchor good feelings for another person too, but again make sure that the anchor is something that can be replicated exactly in terms of position, extent and pressure. A quick tap on the shoulder isn't it!

Have you ever seen the Walt Disney film 'Dumbo'? Can you remember Dumbo's physical anchor? In order to pluck up courage to make his maiden flight, he had to hold a bird feather in his trunk!

---

* By the way, Pavlov's dogs eventually bit the people who rang the bells without providing food. They forget to tell you that bit. (That 'bit'. Get it?)

Classroom anchors

There are lots of ways of using anchors in the classroom – and they work whether students are consciously aware of them or not. You may already be doing some of the following. See if you can identify which bit is the anchor.

Quiet arm

Sit down quietly on your chair and raise your arm for quiet. When any student sees your hand up, they stop talking and raise their own hand until everyone is quiet. (You need to teach this one the first time.)

The penalty box

Always discipline students on or from one special (small) place in the room. This avoids creating unwanted or unintentional negative anchors in different parts of the room, and once the anchor is established you may only need to walk towards the place to stop any minor behavioural problems.

Praise spot

Give praise generously from one particular place too. Make sure you have occasion to use the place regularly, and make sure the praise is genuine and well-deserved. Again, once the anchor is established, just walking to that place can add to the good feeling in the room.

Story time

Have a particular place and format for telling stories. Move your chair to a particular place. Encourage students to sit comfortably. Use a particular tone of voice for the preliminaries. We use the phrase which was always used on the childrens' radio programme: 'Are you sitting comfortably? Then I'll begin.'

Vary your voice tone

In the same way that you can use a particular tone of voice to indicate that a story is imminent, you can use a different tone of voice to get attention and give instructions, another one to signal the end of the lesson, and so on. Use the same form of words to indicate regular activities too.

Homework

Always write up homework assignments on a piece of paper (preferably coloured) and pin it to the same place on the wall.

Plan your blackboard

Keep to a regular format – new vocabulary in a list in one place, instructions somewhere else, etc.

Use colour-coding

Colour-code overhead transparencies, handouts, your board; regular verbs in one colour, irregular verbs in another, etc. Students can use highlighter pens to do this themselves in a reading passage or text. Use colour-coding for correction too.

Timelines: access your past, nourish your future

A **timeline** is a construct of how we represent our present, our future and our past in our minds. Because we all have different 'maps' of time, and experience it differently, we have different timelines.

For some people their past is to their left and their future to their right, or vice versa. Other people might have the future stretching out in front of them and the past behind them, or up and down. They may be on the timeline or off it. Perhaps it runs in a straight line, or curves out in front of them in a semicircle, or some combination of any or all of these. Some move towards the future on their line, the future moves towards others. It can sometimes vary according to what is being imagined and, of course, it is possible to change it.

ESTABLISH
YOUR TIMELINE

Think about something you do every day, preferably something which varies a little (or a lot) from day to day, such as having dinner or going to a class of some sort, rather than cleaning your teeth, which is not likely to be particularly memorable for any specific time.

Now you are going to remember different occasions in the past when you did this thing, and imagine different occasions in the future when you will do it, and think about *where* you imagine each occasion in relation to you. This will give you some idea of how your timeline is constructed. A timeline need not be strictly visual. It might instead (or as well) be auditory or kinaesthetic, involving sounds or feelings rather than pictures. Make sure you get a clear representation of a particular moment each time – and start plotting your timeline. It doesn't hurt and it's fun.

Think about doing the activity – yesterday – two days ago – last weekend – a week ago – a month ago – a year ago – ten years ago.

Think about doing it – now – tomorrow – the day after tomorrow – next weekend – in a week – in a month – in a year – ten years from now.

Alternatively, close your eyes and imagine yourself dissociating from your body and floating upwards. As you look down on yourself from above, have a sense of where your past and present are, where your timeline is.

Are you any the wiser? If not, you may be comforted to know that Jane had trouble establishing her timeline. One day on an NLP course, her partner was rabbiting on about her wavy pink timeline surrounded by white fluffy clouds. Jane suddenly felt inadequate. It obviously was not OK *not* to have a timeline! So she invented one on the spot. It's only a construct anyway. The question is not 'Is it real?' or 'Does it exist?' but rather 'Does it work for me?' or 'Is it useful?'

What can you do with your timeline now you've got it?

You can **take resources from the present and future into the past** in order to soften an unpleasant past memory by giving yourself (and others) resources that were not available at the time.

You can **go along your timeline into your past to collect resources** and bring them back into the present and even take them into the future.

You can **change** it if you don't like it. How? Just do it!

> "If you always do what you've always done, you'll always get what you've always got."
>
> **NLP** ADAGE

- If your past is right in front of you and it's making you miserable, then go inside and put it behind you. (Physically turn round and leave it behind, if you like.)

- If, for example, your future is behind you and you keep thinking to yourself: 'I don't have a future', try putting it in front of you.

- If your past is to your right and your future is to your left and you have problems misreading words, switch your timeline round.

- If you notice that you're off your timeline and you would like to be less detached and more involved in the present, try stepping onto your timeline and have it run through you.

You can always put things back as they were if you're not happy with the changes. Or you can make other changes. As with submodalities, explore, play and notice the differences you get when you do different things. And if what you're doing isn't working … do something else.

TIMELINE TREASURE HUNT

1 Imagine a timeline on the floor, going to your FUTURE in one direction, and your PAST in the other. Establish the present as NOW.

   It doesn't have to correspond exactly with your usual internal timeline, there is no fixed direction, it isn't necessarily a straight line ... you decide.

2 Think of a resource that you would like to have in your life right now. (Energy? Confidence? Self-esteem? Courage? Patience? Optimism? Determination? ...)

3 Take a deep breath and relax. Then step onto your timeline at NOW. You are about to go back into your past and collect instances of the resource you seek.

   You can face your past or your future and walk backwards or forwards – it's up to you. Know that it's OK to get off the timeline at any moment should you feel uncomfortable.

4 Go slowly back down your timeline into the past. Every time you have a sense of encountering your resource, pause and re-experience that event and 'absorb' your resource, before continuing. Get right inside each moment. See what you saw, hear what you heard, feel what you felt. Anchor it, if you wish. (See page 84) Do this until you have had two or three such encounters (or feel that you have gathered enough of your resource).

   Some people have very clear conscious recollections, some have more of an unconscious sense that they have found something. Either way is fine.

5 With your resource, walk up your timeline towards your future. Pause at NOW. Experience having your resource in the present. Then walk onwards into the future, a future enriched by this resource. Pause at any point you know the resource might be particularly useful.

6 Return to NOW, really experience your resource again and bring it back with you as you step off your timeline. Well done.

It *is* a question of having *more* of something rather than building up a resource from scratch. You can also collect a variety of resources on one walk along your timeline. We have all had these resources in some context or other, at some time or another. And when we have experienced something once, we can easily do so again. We just have to know where to find it.

Sir Gawain and the Loathley Lady – PART I

nce upon a time Sir Lancelot was out riding in the forest when he came upon the Black Knight. Sir Lancelot was unarmed, while the Black Knight was carrying an enormous sword.

'If we fought now, I could kill you,' said the Black Knight, 'but I am not an unfair man, so I will give you one chance. I will ask you a question and we will meet here again in one week. If you give me the right answer to the question, I will spare you. If you give me the wrong answer, I will kill you. Do you agree to this?'

Lancelot saw that he had very little choice, so he agreed and he gave the Black Knight his word as a Knight of the Round Table. 'What' he asked 'is the question?'

'The question is this,' sneered the Black Knight. 'What is it that women want?'

'Ah!' thought Lancelot, 'that's a difficult question, but I'll go back to the castle and ask people and between us we're bound to come up with the answer.'

So he set off back to the castle. But on the way he met a horrible, shrivelled up, smelly, totally revolting old hag sitting on a log. 'I know your story,' she slobbered, 'AND I know the answer to the question you must answer.' She cackled so much she ended up having a coughing fit.

'Well, tell me, please,' said Lancelot, trying to be polite.

'I will,' coughed the dreadful old hag, 'if … you take me back to the castle, and if one of the knights marries me.'

Well, Lancelot thought about all the knights and he couldn't somehow imagine any of them being too keen on marrying the hag sitting in front of him. And then the thought came to him that he was a knight himself. And suddenly he remembered that he had to get back to the castle immediately for a very important appointment. He quickly – and very apologetically – made his excuses to the old hag and galloped off as fast as his horse would carry him.

Back at the castle, he started asking people the question: 'What is it that women want?' First he asked Queen Guinevere. She, of all people, was bound to know. But just to be sure, he decided to ask lots of other people too, and see if there was anything they all agreed on. So he asked King Arthur, he asked all the knights, he asked Merlin*, he asked servants, he asked men, he asked women, he even asked children. And every person he asked gave him a different answer: 'beauty', 'love', 'a man', 'children', 'fame', 'chocolates'** …

But that was the problem. There were too many answers. So he decided to sleep on it. Each night he asked himself the question: 'What is it that women want?' And each morning he'd wake up with lots of new suggestions. But none of them seemed to be exactly the right answer.

And the days were passing extraordinarily quickly. Much more quickly than days usually pass.*** And all the time Lancelot kept asking himself, and everyone else he met,

'WHAT IS IT THAT WOMEN WANT?'

---

* Who gave him a sort of magic spell which smelt very nice but which he didn't think the Black Knight would accept.

** Even as he asked the question, he realised that asking a five-year-old was rather optimistic.

*** And he wasn't even tempted to think something clever-clever about how quickly the nights passed. Nights // Knights. Get it?

Communication is non-verbal as well as verbal

Communication is *more* non-verbal than verbal. Research by psychologist Professor Albert Mehrabian shows that 55% of our message is communicated bodily, 38% through our tone of voice, and only 7% through the words we use. When there is a discrepancy between *what* we say (with our words) and *how* we say it (with our body and voice tone), it is the latter which carries more weight. Can you tell whether someone is in a good mood or bad mood before they utter a word? Have you ever heard someone say 'Yes' when you know they really mean 'No'? This mismatch between verbal and non-verbal is sometimes known as **incongruency.**

Mehrabian's research concentrated on the message conveyed in any communication by body language (posture, facial expression, etc) and tone of voice, which was in addition to any words spoken. It was originally conducted by asking American college students the question 'How do you know if someone likes you?' Physical appearance was found to be of critical importance to this group. Mehrabian's research has therefore sometimes been credited with overemphasising the role of physical appearance, and suggesting that you'll *be* OK as long as you *look* OK.

Physical appearance and the way we dress *do* make an important first impression which tends to stick. If the first impression is negative, you may have to work harder at changing it. However, a good first impression, is only that. It obviously makes sense to sound good as well and have something to say too, or the first impression might also be the last!

(Pie chart: Body language 55%, Words 7%, Voice tonality 38%)

Implications

- Be aware of the importance of your own non-verbal communication and aim to be as 'congruent' as you can – make sure your verbal and non-verbal message is the same. Use all three channels (body, voice and words) as fully as possible in your teaching or training, making sure they are working in harmony to convey the same message. Walk the talk.

- Learners of a foreign language need to notice and practise non-verbal as well as verbal interaction and know that they can use all the resources they have (not just linguistic ones) to get their message across. Many learners find this very liberating.

- As teachers we are role models whether we like it or not. Think carefully about your language, gestures, attitudes, appearance and the messages you are giving. You have an impressionable audience.

- When today just isn't your day, admit to students that you 'got out of bed on the wrong side' and apologise in advance for any grumpiness. They should appreciate your honesty – and avoid doing anything to bring your wrath down on their heads!

- Communicate your enthusiasm for teaching and learning in everything you do, and say, and are!

SHOW WITH YOUR BODY

The ability to express meaning clearly through mime or actions is obviously a great asset to a language teacher – or learner. Practise with these emotions.

happy	*sad*	*angry*	*frightened*
bored	*tired*	*impressed*	*unimpressed*
embarrassed	*confident*	*patient*	*amused*
doubtful	*proud*	*alert*	*interested*

Try to be clear and unambiguous; exaggerate if necessary. Remember that we don't all express a particular emotion in the same way. *Your* physical expression of 'boredom' may be different from someone else's: your 'bored' might be confused with someone else's 'thoughtful', for example. Be specially careful about making assumptions about what other people's body posture means. If in doubt … ask! (See also Sensory Acuity page 108)

"Teach your children by what you are, not just by what you say"

⌂ TRANSFER TO TEACHING

This activity, which focuses on adjectives, is an excellent 'pick-me-up' for a tired class. We act the different adjectives and get the students to guess. Then students observe each other and notice similarities and differences between their 'performances'. Students can work in pairs, taking turns to mime adjectives for their partner to guess. We end by asking the whole class to mime 'exhausted', followed by 'alert' and 'interested' and ask them to continue expressing these final two for the rest of the lesson!

How's your voice?

Listen to your voice – on a recording, if necessary. How would you describe it? Sharp? Dull? Monotonous? Interesting? Lively? Grating?

Do your students like to listen to you? Would *you* like to listen to you?

Tips for improving your voice

♦ Take a deep breath before you start speaking.

♦ Breathe with your stomach, not your chest or throat.

♦ Consciously speak slowly and clearly.

♦ Deliberately lower the pitch of your voice.

♦ Use pauses – they enable you to breathe more effectively and they allow others to process what you've just said.

♦ Remember how effective silence can be.

TRANSFER TO TEACHING

These tips will also help students improve their English pronunciation quite noticeably.

Sir Gawain and the Loathley Lady – PART II

o, Sir Lancelot was trying desperately to answer the question: 'What is it that women want?' And he had more answers than he knew what to do with. But none of them seemed to be exactly the answer. And tomorrow was the seventh day when he had to meet the Black Knight again. When he would either give the right answer to the question, or he would die.

In desperation he asked King Arthur to convene a meeting of the Knights of the Round Table. When all the knights were seated, Lancelot explained his problem, his challenge. There was a lot of nodding as the knights realised why Lancelot had been acting so strangely. The room fell silent. Eventually, Sir Gawain coughed and then got up to speak. 'You must keep your word to the Black Knight,' he said, 'but we cannot risk you being killed if you get the answer wrong. You must go back to the old hag and ask her for the answer. And one of us must marry her!'

The room fell silent again. Even the silence fell silent. The knights had never examined their armour quite so intently before. The silence went on being silent. And on. Until finally Sir Gawain coughed again. And in quite a small voice he said, 'I will marry her.'

Lancelot was amazed and deeply moved. 'You would do this for me, Gawain?' he said. 'What a true and loyal friend you are!' 'Yes, a truly true and loyal friend. Well done, Sir Gawain,' said the other knights quickly. 'What a very knightly and courteous thing to do! Three cheers for Sir Gawain!' Back to the forest went Sir Lancelot, and there was the old hag sitting on the same log. The stench was terrible and he had to hold his nose as he got near her.

'My loyal friend, Sir Gawain, has promised to marry you,' he said. 'Pardon?' croaked the old hag. Lancelot let go of his nose and started again. 'My loyal friend, Sir Gawain, has promised to marry you,' he said. The old hag cackled. 'So please,' he said quickly, 'please tell me the answer to the question. What is it that women want?' 'What women want …' she dribbled, 'What women want … is … choice'. 'Choice?' echoed Lancelot, a bit surprised. 'Yes, choice!' snapped the old hag.

'OK, choice, OK.' said Lancelot. 'Thank you very much. Er, I suppose you'd better come with me.' He looked at his horse and he looked at her. 'I don't suppose you fancy a nice walk? Er, no. Of course not.' And with great gallantry he helped her onto his horse (which was not easy as he was holding his nose again). He set off for the castle where preparations for the wedding were already in progress.

The next day, Lancelot rode into the forest to keep his appointment with the Black Knight. The Black Knight sat tall and proud on his horse, nonchalantly swinging his huge sword. 'I've got your answer,' said Lancelot. The Black Knight stiffened slightly and took a firmer hold on his sword. 'I think not, Sir,' he said.

'What women want,' said Lancelot, 'is choice!' The Black Knight's face took on the colour of his armour. He couldn't believe it. He was absolutely astounded. 'How could you possibly know that?' he spluttered.

Lancelot just looked at him, concentrating very hard on keeping his face impassive. 'You may have beaten me this time,' snarled the Black Knight, 'and I'm a man of my word. But we shall meet again, my friend, and next time you might not be so lucky!' And he turned his horse and rode away.

Communication is non-conscious as well as conscious

Jane did her NLP trainer training in the United States. After one of her assessed training sessions, her evaluator said: 'Tell me, Jane. What was your conscious plan for communicating with the non-conscious minds of your audience?'

'Um … Um … Um … I … um … don't think I had one.'

'No,' he said, 'I don't think you had one either. It might be an idea to **have one next time!**'

We tend to believe that unless we learn something consciously, we don't learn it. Unless we know something consciously, we don't know it. Yet has there ever been a time when you've surprised yourself by knowing something without being aware quite how you knew it? According to Dr Emile Donchin at the University of Illinois: more than 99% of our learning is non-conscious.*

We retrieve information non-consciously too. Remember those moments when you try desperately to remember something and you can't? Then as soon as you stop trying and go and make a cup of coffee, it comes back to you? We communicate with ourselves consciously and non-consciously.

> *"If the human brain were so simple that we could understand it, we would be so simple that we couldn't."*
>
> MICHAEL GRINDER

Some thinkers describe us as being two people, the 'conscious me' and the 'non-conscious me'. Usually we're quite good at communicating with the 'conscious me' but less successful when it comes to communicating with the other one. We're not taught how to. In fact, we're often taught not to. Not to go by instinct, intuition, non-conscious feeling, etc. We tend to be told at school that if it can't be proved and justified then it's not valid.

We are avoiding the debate as to whether one side of the brain is associated specifically with the non-conscious mind and the other side with the conscious mind. We don't know, and there doesn't seem to be any proven direct link. What does seem to be true is that learning is more effective when it is multi-sensory and when it appeals to the non-conscious as well as the conscious mind. That's what we're aiming for in this book.

:: **Implications** ::

◆ Trust your non-conscious mind to do things for you and come up with things when you need them – think how well it has looked after you up to now.

◆ Use conscious strategies to facilitate communication with your non-conscious mind, making it easier for it to offer solutions to problems. Relaxation exercises and 'switching off' activities are both helpful here.

◆ Don't try too hard. Take it easy. Trying can be trying!

◆ Consciously try to communicate with the non-conscious minds of your students.

---

* We prefer to use the term 'non-conscious' to 'unconscious' to get away from the unwanted connotations of the latter (knocked out, senseless, unaware).

In the classroom

At first glance it may seem that the major implication of all this is that we teachers are wasting our time. Not so, though what you think you are teaching and what the learners are learning are not necessarily the same. Apparently, as we take in one type of sensory information consciously, we are also taking in information through our other senses non-consciously. So if, for example, we are paying conscious attention with our ears to the words someone is saying, we are also non-consciously noticing what they are doing and what is going on around us with our eyes and our other sense organs.

So what can we do in the classroom about this rather amazing piece of information?

Here are some suggestions. Choose at least three that you could use immediately.

- Make the classroom a sensory-rich learning environment full of things students will take in both consciously and non-consciously.

- On the walls of the classroom have a display of visual material which is both beautiful and informative. Change the display regularly. Enlist students' help.

- Highlight suggestions you want students to follow. In speaking use pauses or changes of voice tone: 'Some people find it really easy to … (pause) … relax.' In writing, you can do it graphologically: What **bold** suggestion did the evaluator make to Jane in the story at the top of the previous page?

- Have songs or music playing while the group is involved in an activity.

- Have frequent changes of activity during lessons, including quiet time when students 'switch off' to allow better non-conscious processing. Such pauses might well be accompanied by music or movement.

- Use storytelling, metaphor, relaxation and guided fantasies.

- Overload students sometimes with more information than the conscious mind can cope with so that the non-conscious mind has to step in and help out.

Miller's 'Seven Plus or Minus Two' theory*

George Miller's 'Seven Plus or Minus Two' theory says that we can only consciously hold in our head around seven bits of information at a time – nine if we are on top form, five if not, or if the information is complicated.

If there are certain items students must remember, present them in groups of five to seven at one time. However an 'item' could be one figure, such as '6', or an easily remembered combination, such as '123', so find ways of linking smaller units to create bigger items.

Contact the non-conscious mind

There are many ways of getting in touch with your non-conscious mind which can enhance your concentration, imagination, creativity and learning potential. Relaxation, meditation, yoga, and physical exercise all help, as does self-hypnosis. Here are some very concrete suggestions for things you, or students, can do, especially before tackling something very challenging or in order to get fresh insights to solve a problem.

---

* In *The Magic Number Seven, Plus or Minus Two* 1956 by American psychologist, George Miller

Pre-view

Whenever you have any creative work to do (eg planning a lesson, writing a report), do a ten-minute overview of the task first. Think about what is involved, what you need to find out, the form the final result will take, etc. Then put it away. You will find that your non-conscious mind is now on the lookout for relevant information and ideas, so be ready to note them down as you think of them. When you come to do the task, you will be ready with some ideas and solutions.

Students might find this approach useful for homework too. Maybe you could allow them a few minutes to preview large homework tasks at the end of class.

We recommend that you use this strategy often. The more you do it and the more you trust your non-conscious mind, the easier it gets. We both find it very effective – especially when we're writing. We don't always get the full answer first time, but each insight helps us to move forward and to state the next request more clearly.*

Information overload

Present 30 items of vocabulary and ask students to learn ten items of their choice.

Information overload not only helps the non-conscious mind, but also makes sense. If you only present five items, students can only learn five items. If you present twenty or thirty items, they may only consciously learn five, or ten, but by sorting through the remainder, they will have a receptive awareness of all the words, making it much easier to learn them next time.

 CONSCIOUS COUNTDOWN

1   Think about a particular issue or problem for which you would like some insight or a possible solution.

2   Mentally ask your non-conscious mind to help out with this issue. Close your eyes and state your request clearly to your non-conscious mind.

3   Count backwards out loud from 1000 to 927. This is to distract the conscious mind. If 1000 to 927 is too easy, count from 10,000 to 9,927! Or look at a mandala (see page 10) or do the NLP alphabet activity on the next page.

4   When you have finished, be aware of anything at all that comes to mind. And it doesn't matter if what comes to mind seems to have nothing whatever to do with your issue. The more irrelevant it seems to be, the more relevant it is likely to be. What new light, if any, has been shed on your issue?

 TRANSFER TO TEACHING

Ask students to think about an issue in relation to learning (English or anything else) – this might be a particular learning difficulty, lack of time to study – anything. Before mentally addressing their non-conscious mind, students should work with a partner and each write a specific request for help, stating clearly what they want. After doing steps 3 and 4, students exchange thoughts with their partner and help to interpret each other's thoughts.

---

  * If you want to know more about the wonderful ways of communicating with the non-conscious mind, read about the work of the famous hypno-therapist Milton Erickson, eg in Alman and Lambrou's *Self Hypnosis*. (See booklist)

NLP ALPHABET*

Write out a large copy of the alphabet like this and pin it on the wall:

A	B	C	D	E	F	G	H	I
L	R	L	B	R	R	L	B	R

J	K	L	M	N	O	P	Q	R
B	L	R	B	R	L	L	R	B

S	T	U	V	W	X	Y	Z
B	R	L	R	R	B	L	R

As you read the letters of the alphabet aloud, simultaneously respond to the letters underneath as follows:

L   Raise your *left* hand (and right knee)

R   Raise your *right* hand (and left knee)

B   Raise *both* hands (and jump in the air)

It's not as easy as it sounds and involves total concentration. Two of the benefits of this activity are improved concentration and physical co-ordination. The first time just raise your hands. Once you've got the idea, add in the leg movements.

TRANSFER TO TEACHING

This is a novel way of practising the alphabet. Prepare two or three variations of this alphabet by altering the distribution of L, R and B. Students work in different groups, and if anyone seems to have perfected their responses, move them to a different alphabet. You can also ask them to read the alphabet backwards, starting with Z. Or work up and down the columns.

THINK

Put these in order – from 'not knowing' to 'knowing':**

a) Conscious incompetence   = I know I don't know

b) Non-conscious competence   = I know without thinking

c) Conscious competence   = I know I know – if I think about it

d) Non-conscious incompetence = I don't know I don't know

---

*   Adapted from Grinder and DeLozier's 'New Code' NLP

**   d – a – c – b

Look at a mandala

Look at the mandala on page 10. Hold it or place it on a table a comfortable distance away and fix your eyes on the very centre of it.

Stare at the centre of the mandala for about 3 minutes. As you do so, just be aware of your own breathing. You will probably have a sense of lines moving in and out of focus as you stare. This is normal. If a conscious thought comes into your mind, that's fine too. Acknowledge it and let it float away or put it into a mental dustbin.

Do this for two or three minutes to start with. Do it daily, gradually increasing the amount of time until you are up to about six or seven, or even ten minutes – whatever is comfortable. You should notice an improvement in your ability to concentrate, and find it easier to access ideas from your non-conscious mind.

 TRANSFER TO TEACHING

Give each student a copy of the mandala. Teach the words blink and swallow, and tell students that they can do both during the activity as described. Using Magic Eye pictures has a similar mesmerising and centring effect. Be careful, though. It can be quite frustrating for those who can't do it – yet!

Isn't this hypnosis?

Some people are nervous of words like 'hypnosis' and 'trance'. Some of the activities we suggest may seem like hypnosis. So we thought you'd like to be reassured.

We all go into trances regularly, perfectly naturally and without ill effect. We call it 'daydreaming', 'going blank' for a moment, 'switching off'. Have you ever been driving a car and suddenly realised that you can't remember actually driving the last few miles? You were off 'in another world', and yet you know that a part of your brain was still monitoring your surroundings and making sure that you were driving safely. So it is with trance or hypnosis. You are not unconscious. Often you are hyper-aware of what is going on. Always there is a part of your brain which is checking on your physical and psychological safety. No-one can hypnotise you without your consent and no-one can make you do something which conflicts with your values and beliefs. So-called 'brainwashing' can apparently be achieved, but only with very extreme measures, such as physical or mental torture – which you would certainly notice!

Hypnosis, whether self induced or aided by someone else, is simply a process of relaxing so that your non-conscious mind can communicate with you more effectively, and positive suggestions can register more clearly. Because the non-conscious mind is benevolent (another NLP presupposition), it will accept only those suggestions which are in your own best interests, and filter out the rest. The more you understand about positive suggestions and relaxation, the less control other people can have over you without your knowledge and consent. The more you practise the techniques of making positive suggestions to yourself in a way that will bring you most benefit, the more control you will have over your own life.

Sir Gawain and the Loathley Lady – PART III

he day of the wedding dawned bright and sunny at the castle. The old hag was given a bath – several baths – all with soap and bath oils and bubble bath with lots and lots of bubbles, but she still smelt disgusting. She was given the most gorgeous gown to wear, made of lace and silk and covered with precious jewels. But she still looked absolutely revolting, and even the veil didn't help much.

The ceremony took place. And then everyone joined the happy couple – well, the couple – to celebrate. And everyone danced and ate and drank … and made very careful speeches.

And eventually the time came when Gawain could no longer put off going to the bedchamber with his monstrous bride. They went inside and he spent a very long time closing the door. Behind him he heard the creak as she jumped up onto the huge four-poster bed. And he heard the rustle as she began to take off her clothes – with far too much enthusiasm, it seemed to him.

Gawain felt faint. He couldn't bear to look. Then he heard her say, 'Darling, come to bed. Come and hold me in your arms.' Gawain reminded himself that he was a knight, used to facing dreadful trials. He reminded himself that he was used to vanquishing dragons and other monsters. Then he quickly reminded himself that he couldn't deal with this one in the usual way. So he reminded himself that he was doing this to save the life of his friend and fellow knight. He took a deep breath, said a quick prayer and turned round. And there on the bed was the most beautiful woman he had ever seen in his life.

'Wow!' he exclaimed.

And then he suddenly remembered the hag and looked round the room.

'It's me. I am her … she! It is I,' she said. 'What I mean is, I am the same woman you married today.' And then she explained that she had offended a wicked witch who was jealous of her beauty. And the witch had put her under a spell which made her look old and ugly and repulsive. The spell could only be broken by marrying a knight. 'You, Gawain, are that knight. You have broken the spell.'

'Gosh!' said Gawain, who seemed to have forgotten all his knightly vocabulary. He couldn't believe his good fortune.

'At least,' said his bride. 'There is just one thing. I'm afraid the spell is not completely broken. The witch told me that upon my marriage I would lead a split life. For twelve hours every day I will be the woman you see before you now. But for the other twelve hours, I must be the old hag you married. So, which would you prefer? Would you like me to be beautiful during the day and ugly at night, or ugly during the day and beautiful at night?'

Gawain thought about this for a moment or two. He looked into the eyes of his beautiful young wife and imagined her by day. And then he imagined her by night. He thought back to the ugly hag and didn't want to imagine her by day or by night. And then he remembered, truly remembered, that he was a good and honest knight. And at that moment he knew the answer. And he spoke the words that broke the spell completely and forever.

The use of metaphor

In NLP, we do not use the word 'metaphor' in quite the same way as it is used in the study of Literature. What we mean is 'an indirect communication by a word, expression or story which implies similarities between things or events'. Or, put more simply, 'X is like Y'.

Metaphor in NLP by-passes the conscious mind and gives us direct access to the non-conscious mind. It's a wonderful way of giving indirect advice or making an indirect suggestion to someone. The conscious mind might well reject or refute advice, but it can't really object to you telling a story. So the non-conscious mind is free to consider the messages of the story. A metaphor is by its very nature ambiguous, and open to interpretation. If you are in good rapport with a person, their non-conscious mind will interpret the story in the way which is most beneficial to them. This will give the person new options about what to do to change their situation. They will almost certainly have considered – and rejected – many conscious options. The non-conscious mind, though, is likely to reveal itself as a flash of inspiration, a sudden new perspective on the situation; something the person has thought of all by themselves – so resist the impulse to point out your role! What is important is that you've helped. People will eventually – non-consciously – come to realise that they feel better when you are around, so you'll get your reward in the long-term!

"Her eyes were like Christmas puddings — deep brown, rich and spicy and full of hidden gifts."

The simplest level of metaphor is to tell a story about 'your friend'. 'A friend of mine had a problem like that. He tried [… insert possible course of action …] and found it really helpful.' It's a bit obvious, but it's better than 'Why don't you … ?'

A more subtle approach is to tell a story which has the same structure as your friend's problem situation, but where the link is less obvious. All the fairy stories we tell our children to lull them to sleep are pale imitations of the originals. They were much more frightening because they were telling children about the possible consequences of their actions. (Susan's father used to tell the more worthy, less comfortable versions. Goldilocks ended up at the police station for breaking and entering. Hansel and Gretel deserved to be locked up by the witch because they'd run away from home and stolen bits off her roof!)

"Men are like buses — you wait ages for the right one, then three arrive at the same time!"

So, you might perhaps – depending on the age and interests of the person – tell a story about a bunny rabbit, or a computer firm! Decide on the message you want to give, and think of an imaginary situation to turn into a story. We are not suggesting that you start by setting up an advice centre. However, story-telling is a powerful tool both inside and outside the language classroom.

 CHOOSE A METAPHOR

Complete the following sentences:

Teaching English is like …

Learning is like …

My job is like …

Now go back and give at least two other possibilities for each of the sentences. Which one is the most relevant or helpful to you?

Diana Beaver, the author of *Lazy Learning*, gets her students to use a metaphor for themselves as learners. Her own metaphor is to think of herself as a sea otter learning through play as she works on her research, and when she works with groups, as a fountain constantly replenishing its energy as a source for others. Here are some metaphors for teaching and learning English that Susan uses:

- Learning English is like doing a 1,000-piece jigsaw puzzle: you have an overview of the picture you're aiming at and you've got lots of individual pieces. At the beginning it's quite difficult to put them together, but gradually whole areas become clear. Sometimes you find that a chunk needs to be moved and then a lot of other things slot into place. And even when you've got a lot of the picture, there always seems to be that huge area of sky you can't quite get to grips with.

- Teaching English is like using the zoom lens on a camera: you pull back to show the whole frame, then you zoom right down onto one specific bit of language. Then pull back to show how it fits together with things around it.

- Learning English is like a journey that students and teacher take together. Each person starts from a slightly different place but you're all making for the same destination. Sometimes you take a short cut to reach a particular goal quickly. Sometimes you have time to wander and enjoy the scenery and each other's company. Sometimes someone goes off down their own particular side alley, but they come back and join the group again. And in the process you get to know each other very well.

What are your metaphors?

How do they change your perspective on teaching and learning?

Stories and guided fantasies

Stories and guided fantasies are wonderful vehicles for delivering powerful and empowering metaphors to your students and to yourself.

How you tell a story can greatly add to its power. Try telling part of a story at the beginning of a lesson, stopping at a suitable, tantalising point, and finishing it at the end of the lesson. This distracts the conscious mind as it tries to make sense of the story and searches for an ending, which frees up the non-conscious mind to process the story in other ways.

If you are inventing guided fantasies it is important to give enough information for students to be able to begin to imagine the scene, but not so much that you disrupt and contradict what they are imagining. To help give free rein to their imagination it is a good idea to *use general rather than specific words* as far as possible, and to give them plenty of choices, such as 'Imagine you are walking in a forest surrounded by wonderful trees. Imagine the colours of the trees.' This is better than saying, 'Imagine you are walking in a dark forest surrounded by green pine trees …'.

Place embedded commands in the stories and guided fantasies. These also by-pass the conscious mind and are taken up by the non-conscious mind. How do you embed a command? You can either put it into inverted commas, ie direct speech, as in *'And the fairy said to the princess, **"You can do anything you like"**.'* Or you can mark it out by using a pause or a change of voice tone. (See the point about highlighting suggestions on page 96) Be aware of the embedded commands that are in your stories. Make sure that you **communicate positive, empowering sentiments to your students!**

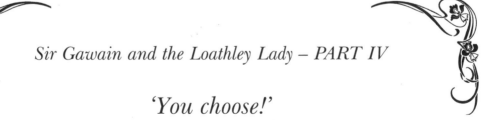

Sir Gawain and the Loathley Lady – PART IV

'You choose!'

A journey

The purpose of this induction is to relax you, to build up your resources and to orient you towards the future with confidence.

When you listen to a double induction – two voices speaking to you at the same time – it is very hard to concentrate on either one of them alone. Your conscious mind becomes overloaded and confused. *This is the whole point.* After a while, your conscious mind will give up the effort of trying to make sense of everything it hears, and your non-conscious mind will take over the receptive process, and *benefit from it hugely,* selecting those meanings which are of greatest value to you.

For this reason, we suggest that you don't read the texts before you listen. (Don't think of a hippo on a trampoline!) We thought very hard about not printing them at all, but decided to do so in the end, for those of you who feel you really must (must?) *see* what you are getting before you hear it or before you use it with students. We do advise you, however, to *just listen* … and *enjoy it* and *trust your non-conscious mind to cope with it wonderfully.*

Guided fantasy: A journey

Make sure you're sitting comfortably with both feet flat on the floor. Take a deep breath in and let it go. And relax.

We're going on a journey, so close your eyes and step confidently onto the path which leads into the forest. You know you're safe and you're ready for all the new things you'll meet along the way. As you walk, feel the ground beneath your feet and the refreshing cool breeze on your face. Really appreciate everything you can see and hear and feel around you. Appreciate your journey every step of the way. You can hear the rustle of the wind in the leaves and the sound of birds singing as they fly high in the sky. And from somewhere the sound of running water.

Look around you and see the trees - there's one here close by. You can see it clearly standing tall and strong and it reminds you of something. Something from your past. A time when you felt strong. And you feel that strength again.

And there are more trees growing all around. Many different varieties. Different shapes. Different colours. Tall and short. Old trees that have been there a very long time and some new young saplings beginning to

Relax. Just relax. A long journey. Always remembering that the longest journey begins with a single step. The ground is there to support you. To give you support. The breeze is there to refresh you and lighten your load.

As you walk just be aware of all the things that you can see and hear and feel. And those birds, watching them fly, and knowing that you too can fly. You can fly. And the trees are there all around you, rooted to the ground throwing their roots down and down, and using them to take from the earth goodness and moisture and nutrients, and taking those things up and through the trunk, and up and through the branches and out to the green leaves, allowing them to grow full and rich and green and lush.

shoot. Some you know the names of. Many you recognise. And some are totally new to you.

And there are openings between the trees. Opportunities for you so see through and beyond. In one of the openings you glimpse something moving. You wonder what it is. You're positive it's something exciting and intriguing. You move towards it. You have to push your way through some bushes. It isn't quite so easy to walk here, but you're inspired by the desire to find out what it was you saw. There's a final tangle of undergrowth which blocks your view entirely, and you feel a moment of doubt. You look back, and you can see the tree you saw before, the tall strong tree, your tree. And you feel again your own strength returning and you decide to go ahead. And as soon as you make the decision, you move ahead confidently and it's actually quite easy to get through the undergrowth and suddenly you're through and you find yourself in a clearing with the sun breaking through. You look round, and you see a movement again, just beyond the trees at the edge of the clearing. And as you move towards the new opening, you see something on the ground, glinting in the sun. You look more closely and bend down and pick up - a key. You examine the key and turn it round in your hands. You may wonder what the key will open. You nay know what the key will open. Whatever the case you know it's a key for you. And you realise that this is something very special, something precious, something magic.

Looking round again you see a path leading out of the clearing, a short cut which will take you back home. You know the way to come back to this place again. So, feeling relaxed and refreshed, take the path which brings you home. And when you're ready, put your hands over your face and gently open your eyes.

Open. Be open, Be open to learning. Be curious. Ask questions. Questions, questions, questions. And know that you can walk. That you can know. That deep within you, like the trunk of a tree, are all the resources that you need to do the things that you want to do.

And know that you can be strong. Just decide, knowing that whatever you decide the decision will be right for you. Because you know, you do know, that your non-conscious mind looks after you in the way that it's always done and the way that it always will do.

Something shining. Something sparkling. Something... interesting. A key for you. A key to open something. A key to something that you can open, and find out its secrets. The answer perhaps to a question, a question that you're asking.

Something special. Something key. Something that you know can take you on a new journey. Relaxed. And refreshed. With the key in your mind, knowing that the key is there.

All behaviour has a positive intention

'Positive' here does not mean 'good' so much as 'goal-driven'. In other words, whatever we do, we do for a purpose. This does not mean that the positive intention of what I do is positive for *you,* but it is for *me.* In some way. And if ever I want to change something I do, the only way I shall succeed is by making sure that when I drop the behaviour, I don't drop the positive intention too. I have to safeguard the positive intention by doing something else that satisfies it, or I will always go back to the old behaviour.

"Don't throw out the baby with the bath water!"

Jane gave up smoking many, many times and always started again. Living in a non-smoking household, she used to go into the garden to smoke. She realised one day that smoking gave her a rare and delicious chance to be alone. Only when she found other ways of being alone was she able to stop smoking for good.

This presupposition is also crucial if you hope to change someone else's behaviour. You need to know what the positive intention behind the behaviour is and help them to find another way of satisfying it, before they will be able to get rid of the old behaviour. Try to give people – and yourself – other choices. Very rarely are people deliberately behaving in a way to make you miserable. Remember another NLP presupposition:

People make the best choice available to them at the time.

Implications

Dealing with disruption

If someone is disruptive in lessons, find out what need their disruptive behaviour is satisfying and help them to satisfy it by doing something different, which isn't disruptive. If it's a need for attention, try suggesting alternative ways of getting your attention, or make them the spokesperson for a group, or ask them to undertake a special task, or whatever. Maybe the task is not challenging enough for them and they're bored. Add an extra dimension to the task to make it more challenging. There may be another reason. Whatever it is, find out and act on it.

Reframing

Remember reframing? (See page 49) There are two sides to every character trait, so since you can't change the students, try changing your response. Try viewing all your students positively. The *bossy* student probably has excellent *leadership qualities.* Maybe *sullen* is just *thoughtful.*

See what you can do with: (a) nosy (b) weird (c) noisy (d) picky*

SUGGESTED ANSWERS

---

* (a) curious (b) unique (c) enthusiastic (d) careful, meticulous

FIND THE POSITIVE INTENTIONS

If you are already perfect, you can skip this activity.

If there is something you want to change in your life, you need to find out the positive benefit of your behaviour and find something you are happy to do that will give you that same benefit. That in itself might be enough to enable you to make a change. However, there are three things to note:

a) What you consciously think the positive intention is might not be the main benefit. You may need to access this information from your non-conscious mind.

b) If it proves to be too difficult to find new behaviour which safeguards the positive intention of the old, you may decide to stick with the old.

c) Once you are aware of the positive intention, you may decide not to change the behaviour anyway!

Try the following, though. It often works.

1   Think of something you do, that you wish you didn't do, something you would really like to change, eg biting your fingernails, eating or drinking too much, smoking, grinding your teeth, being late, laughing too loudly, saying inappropriate things, tidying up obsessively, leaving things in a mess …

2   Consciously think of two or three possible reasons why this behaviour is useful to you, eg it relaxes you, stops you feeling nervous, helps you feel independent, stops you doing something even worse!

3   Now ask your non-conscious mind to give you some possible reasons why this behaviour is useful to you. Do the 'Conscious Countdown' on page 97.

4   What ideas came to mind? Yes, that one! Very often the most bizarre and seemingly irrelevant ideas, the ones that we immediately reject, are in fact the crucial ones.

5   Consciously think of five different things you could do instead of the behaviour in 1 to satisfy the needs in 2 and 4.

6   Now ask your non-conscious mind for some ideas, as you did in 3.

7   Now that you have all that useful information, is there anything you'd like to start doing now?

Sensory acuity: noticing, not assuming

Sensory acuity is the third pillar of NLP and the third phase of the Basic Action Model: 'Notice the response'. (See page 17) It is concerned with noticing the non-verbal clues that people are communicating to us all the time. *Noticing, not assuming.* Noticing something is different from interpreting or making an assumption about what you have noticed.

When I assume I make an 'ass' out of 'u' and 'me'!

In the same way that we already have rapport skills, we already have sensory acuity. We know that when someone says 'Yes' in a certain tone of voice, with a certain intonation, a certain facial expression and a certain shrug of their shoulders, what they really mean is 'No'. We have had years of practice at picking up on people's non-verbal messages and we do so unconsciously. NLP brings to consciousness some of these automatic skills so we can use them more skilfully.

Be careful not to assign a direct one-to-one meaning to every posture. A person with folded arms *might* be feeling defensive, but might equally be feeling a whole lot of other things: relaxed, happy, open to ideas – or even cold or just comfortable! We cannot assume what it means in this particular instance or that it means the same thing on every occasion. Nor can we assume that because it means one thing for one person that it means the same thing for everyone – or anyone – else.

So how can we know? We can look, we can guess and we can ask. With practice we're likely to get better at guessing correctly, but rather than ascribe motives to people that they may not have had, check it out with them. In NLP, we are trying to become *more* sensitive to other people's signals, not less.

So start practising. Notice your own body language and notice how you are feeling when you adopt certain postures. Be aware of the signals you are giving with your body language and make sure they are the signals you want to give. Become aware of the postures other people adopt while they are expressing certain emotions. You might find it easier to watch people you are not actually talking to, or to watch people on television. Watch actors too. Do you believe in the emotions they are portraying? You do if they're good. What are they doing? How are they doing it?

One good way of sensing how another person is feeling is to match their breathing, and then to notice how you begin to feel yourself, though if they are in some kind of 'negative' state, you may not wish to do so for very long.

:: **Implications** ::

◆ Practise your sensory acuity and really notice things. The more observant you are, the more skilled you will be at getting into rapport with other people.

◆ Be alert to the non-verbal signals your learners give and respond accordingly. If you notice that all

is not well with one student (or several or all of them) then do something about it right away.

◆ Heed your intuition here. Very often what we sense intuitively is spot on. If you sense something is wrong, you're probably right. But always remember the golden rule: *When in doubt, ask!*

 WHICH HAND?

Ask a volunteer friend to hide a coin in one hand. Your job is to guess which hand the coin is in. Ask the person to concentrate on the hand holding the coin and not to do anything knowingly to help you or hinder you.

When you have guessed correctly five times in a row, ask them to deliberately try to mislead you. When you get good at that, ask them either to try to help or to mislead, but not to tell you which. Don't forget to let them have a go too.

 TRANSFER TO TEACHING

This is a lovely pairwork activity for students. Get the 'guesser' to write down the clues they are noticing which give the game away (and not to tell their partner until they have both had a go). Finish the activity with feedback from the whole class giving linguistic input where necessary.

 POSITIVE STATE /
NEGATIVE STATE

1 Ask your friend to remember a time – in silence – when they had a really good experience, and to 'go inside', close their eyes and re-experience it. Notice anything you can about the person's facial expression and body language: changes in skin colour, movements around the mouth or eyes or in the jaw, hands or feet, head or shoulder movements, changes in breathing, eye movement …

2 Ask them to let that go and 'break state'. (See page 20)

3 Next ask them to remember a time – in silence – when something didn't go as they wanted it to and to re-experience it. Again, notice anything you can.

Ask them not to choose a real tragedy! Suggest they use some conflict or disappointment at work or place of study. Don't let them stay too long in this negative experience. Ask them to break state as soon as you've seen it.

4 Be aware of the differences you noticed between the two states.

5 Now ask your friend to choose one of the two experiences – without telling you which one it is – and re-experience it. Is it the good experience or the bad one? Try to get it right three times in a row. Break state between each experience, or you may get emotion from one state 'contaminating' the other.

6 Let them try too.

Variations

You could add a third, neutral experience. You could also add the element of voice. Ask your volunteer to relive either the good or the bad experience and, at the same time, to count from one to ten while you shut your eyes. Judge which state it is from listening carefully to the tone and quality of the voice.

 TRANSFER TO TEACHING

Demonstrate the activity first with a volunteer in front of the class as this will make the instructions clear and also give you the opportunity to pre-teach useful language. Have students work in groups of three: one volunteer and two observers – two heads are often better than one in this type of activity.

Rapport: the key to communication

Rapport* is one of the four pillars of NLP and, according to one of the NLP presuppositions, 'Rapport is the key to successful communication and to influence.'

What exactly is rapport? According to the dictionary it is 'a harmonious or sympathetic relation or connection'. It might also be defined as 'meeting someone at their map of the world'. Or we could say maximising similarities and minimising differences between people at the non-conscious level. Sometimes it concerns sharing beliefs, values and goals with a person. Sometimes it's just sharing a joke. With some people we find it happens easily and spontaneously. With others we have to work harder, or more consciously, which is where NLP can help.

THINK

How do we establish rapport with one another?

♦ How can you tell that two people are in love (and therefore very much in rapport with one another)? What is it about them? What do they do?

♦ When you meet someone new at a party, what sort of things do both of you say and do in order to build rapport?

♦ Think about someone you really like and feel comfortable with. What's going on? Why do you feel comfortable? What are you both doing?

♦ Now ask yourself the same questions about someone you don't like and/or don't feel comfortable with. How does it show to other people?

Matching and mirroring

Have you ever watched good friends in a café and noticed how they match and mirror each other physically? They will tend to be sitting in similar positions: perhaps they will both have their legs crossed and one elbow on the table, chin in hand. If one changes position, eg leans forward, chin in hand, it is likely that in a moment or two, the other will do the same.

Matching is doing the same thing with the same part of the body as the other person ie crossing your right leg over your left leg to match them crossing their right leg over their left leg.

Mirroring is using the opposite side of your body as in a mirror, eg putting your right hand behind your head when they put their left hand behind their head.

This **body matching** is something we can do consciously with anyone, in order to facilitate communication. Just observe how the person is standing or sitting and take up more or less the same position. (Match their position not their gestures. The gestures of the speaker are often inappropriate for the listener!)

---

* Pronounced ra-pore, without the 't', more or less like the French original.

There are other ways we can match too. We can match a person's **voice,** for example, which can be very useful for putting someone at ease on the telephone. Just approximate to their speed, tone and pitch.

We also match their speed and depth of **breathing** and their general level of alertness. If someone is animated and moving a lot, look alert and interested. If they are calm and still, excessive fidgeting on your part could be irritating.

Perhaps you're wondering: 'But won't people notice if I match their body or voice? And mightn't they think I'm making fun of them?' If she isn't careful, Susan has a bad habit of picking up people's accents when she's talking to them, which can sound as if she's making fun of them and does not lead to rapport. But, no, people don't usually consciously notice body matching, because it's something everyone does automatically when they are in good rapport. As long as you are careful to match and not mimic, people should just get a sense of being understood and appreciated. If someone ever does seem to notice and be offended by your matching then the solution is quite simple. Remember the NLP Basic Action Model on page 17? Stop doing what you're doing and do something else!

If you are worried about being too obvious, then it is possible to **cross-match.** For example, instead of matching a person's breathing by breathing in the same way, you can tap your finger gently in time with their breathing, or move your foot in time with their speaking. As long as you are genuinely trying to establish rapport with the person, you should find a lot of this happening naturally. This really is a natural process at all levels. People who want to establish group identity match at the level of dress, interest, language, culture, beliefs and values. Just watch any group of teenagers – or even bankers!

Don't take our word for any of this. Look around you and see what you see. Watch people who are obviously in rapport and those who aren't. Watch how groups establish their identity. Explore these ideas and find out what happens. Body match a person you're with. What effect does it have? Voice match someone on the phone. What effect does it have? And try mismatching too in either situation. What effect does that have?

THINK

What makes a good listener?

Jot down notes on the things a good listener says or does ... and the things a good listener doesn't say or do.*

* Make eye contact; encouraging facial expression; head nods; full attention; body matching (see above); cross matching (see above); body position (alert, leaning slightly forwards, etc); empathetic noises such as 'Mm', 'Oh', 'Ah', etc; interjections such as 'Really?', 'Oh dear', 'How awful', 'What a bummer!' etc; repetition of key words – their original words, not your interpretation of their words (this needs to be done sparingly, but can sometimes be helpful); questions to check you've really understood what they mean or to elicit further information: 'So what you're saying is ...', 'Do you mean that ...?', 'Tell me more ...' etc.

Matching predicates

Another way to get into rapport with someone is to listen carefully to their sensory-specific language ... and to use language from the same representational system back to them. (See page 42) NLP calls this 'matching predicates'. So if, for example, you notice that another person is using a lot of visual language, then by using visual language yourself, you are maximising similarities and minimising differences with them on yet another level.

If they say, 'It doesn't sound very clear to me', you might say, 'Well let me spell it out for you.' (Both are auditory.) Conversely of course, mismatching predicates can lead to less effective communication. What systems are A and B using in the following? Which predicates tell you this?

A *I'm under a lot of pressure. I feel really weighed down by it all.*

B *Can't you see any light on the horizon at all?*

A *No, it's all on top of me at the moment.**

Listening skills

Perhaps the most basic component of rapport is the ability to listen. We're very good at talking. Many of us are not so good at listening. When someone is telling us about the dreadful experience they've just had, we're very quick to jump in and tell them about the even more dreadful experience that we've had. It is more helpful and respectful if we just soothe, empathise, reassure and ... listen.

The Chinese verb 'to listen'

ear

eyes

heart

The next time you are having a conversation, practise your listening skills. Resist the temptation to give all your news, and listen attentively to what the other person is telling you. Try to use as many as possible of the techniques from the previous pages. Notice the response you get. (It's amazing how people think that good listeners are 'intelligent'!) If you're in any doubt, come clean. Tell the other person what you're trying to do – before you start doing it. Ask for feedback.

 TRANSFER TO TEACHING

Teach and encourage good listening skills when others are talking. Make it an explicit part of the activity that everybody listens with full attention during the telling of stories or anecdotes.

———————————————— SUGGESTED ANSWERS ————————————————

* A = kinaesthetic (pressure, feel, weighed down, on top of me) B = visual (see, light, horizon)

The structure of influence

Matching is very powerful. Once we match we can begin to influence, if we choose to, and if it's appropriate. In fact we can only influence from a matching position – from a position of rapport. It's no good shouting at someone if you don't like what they're doing. We've all tried that and it tends to be counter-productive. If we want someone to change their behaviour, first of all we have to pace them and appreciate where they're at. Only then can we begin to lead them somewhere different. This goes for state of mind as well as body, and, as we have seen, the two are connected. Someone who is depressed, for example, will not usually respond well to jollying up or to being told to snap out of it. They need a bit of sympathy first.

An English teacher in the Basque country told about his experience with a class of 16-year-old boys he found very difficult to motivate and teach. The teacher thought that if he could somehow reach the 'leader' of the class – who would always sit sprawled back in his chair, legs stretched out, arms folded, chewing gum – he would get the class as a whole to open up a bit. This teacher knew about matching and he felt he had nothing to lose.

One day, before the class began, he sat down next to the young man … in exactly the same position (but without the gum). He started talking about this and that, things he knew to be of interest, and little by little, he changed his position and gradually became more upright. And after a while, the young man also began slowly to shift his position to a more upright one. And with the change in body posture there came a change in attitude and behaviour. Not a revolutionary one, but certainly the beginnings of one. And from then on things in that class were a little bit different.

What the English teacher did with the teenager in his class is called **'pacing and leading'**, and it fits into a model known as **The Structure of Influence:**

The English teacher first 'paced' his student by matching body posture and topics of interest. He did this for quite a while and then he eventually 'led' the student somewhere else by changing his own body posture so that the student followed.

You could also pace and lead someone by matching (or approximating) their breathing or their voice or their general level of movement … and then gradually changing yours. If a person doesn't follow your lead, it is probably because you haven't paced them enough. So go back and pace some more – possibly in a different or an additional way – before attempting to lead again.

THINK

Many of the things described in this section on rapport are obviously applicable on a one-to-one basis. Before you read on, think how you could apply any of them to the classroom situation.

Implications

♦ You obviously can't match and mirror a whole class at the same time but you can get them all into rapport with each other by doing an action song or chant, for example. Not only does this ensure that everyone is matching everyone else, but it also gets everybody breathing in time: both physiological and respiratory rapport. Dancing a dance with specific steps (circle dancing and line dancing, for example) also has this effect, as do certain mime games like 'Simon says …'

♦ In cases where there is a distinct group mood of general discontent, tiredness, silliness etc, then pace whatever the mood is by saying something like: 'OK. I notice a mood of silliness. So let's do a really silly activity!' or 'You seem to be getting a bit tired. Would you like to do a relaxation exercise to have a little rest and raise your energy level?'

♦ As for matching predicates, you can monitor your own language to check that it is not specific to the same sensory rep system all the time and to make sure you use a variety of predicates from different systems. Secondly you can use neutral language some of the time, so that for instance instead of saying 'I see that …' or 'I feel that …', you say 'I think that …' and so on.

♦ A group is composed of individuals who are often experiencing different things. One way of pacing these differences is to take a moment from time to time just to check where everyone is, maybe by asking them to give an adjective to describe their state of mind. This allows you and the students to get a sense of everyone's mood, acknowledge the different feelings and follow anything up if there is a problem.

The monster and the watermelon

nce upon a time a traveller rode his horse down a hill into a village. He saw a large group of villagers up ahead looking into a field and shouting and waving their arms. As the traveller came closer some of the villagers ran up to him shouting: 'Help! Help! There's a monster in there!'

The traveller looked into the field. The only thing he could see was a watermelon. 'Don't be silly,' he said. 'It's not a monster. It's a watermelon.' They villagers didn't like to be told this. 'It's a monster!' they shouted. 'No, it isn't,' said the traveller. The villagers were getting angry. 'It's a monster!' they shrieked. 'No, it isn't,' shouted the exasperated traveller. 'Anyone can see it's a watermelon!' The villagers were incensed. They dragged the traveller off his horse and threw him into the duck pond.

Later that day – long after the first traveller had crawled out of the duck pond and ridden away dripping and squelching – another traveller rode down the same hill. The group of villagers was still up ahead, looking into the same field and shouting and waving their arms. As the traveller came closer some of the villagers ran up to him shouting: 'Help! Help! There's a monster in there!' The traveller looked into the field.

'So there is!' he yelled. He drew his sword, spurred his horse, jumped over the gate and galloped across the field, slashing away in all directions. There were bits of watermelon everywhere. As he cantered back again the villagers cheered with relief and delight. They were so pleased, that they invited the traveller to stay with them for a while. So he did.

He learned a lot from them about their way of life and how they did things in that part of the world. And he listened to their stories with great interest and attention. And in turn, he told them stories too. And he taught them things that he knew about. One of the things he taught them – little by little – was the difference between a monster and a watermelon.

The day came for the traveller to leave and the villagers accompanied him to the edge of the village. As they passed the watermelon field, the villagers pointed into the field and laughed as they said: 'There's a watermelon in there!'

'Yes, there is,' said the traveller. 'And sometimes there's a monster in there too!'

And he winked and went on his way.

Perceptual positions: see it my way, see it your way

A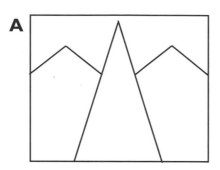

B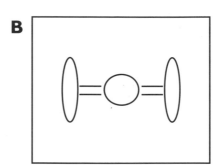

Look again!

What happens when you look at these drawings from different angles?
What do you see when you look at them as though from head on?
What do you see when you look at them as though from above?
What do you see when you look at them as though from below?
Some of our own, sometimes zany, ideas are given at the bottom of the page.*

What is the point of this? The point is that if you look at things from different angles, they change. Or rather, they don't change, your perception of them changes. And the same is true of different perceptual positions. Different positions give us different information, and this can be very useful when we're trying to solve a problem or get on better with other people.

One way of getting a different perspective on a relationship or problem, is to do exactly that. See it from a different position. Hear another argument. Feel what it's like from the other side.

"Do not judge a person until you have walked many moons in their moccasins."

NLP offers a clear technique for viewing things from at least three different points of view, called **perceptual positions.** We each tend to favour one of these positions. But really good communicators have the ability to switch easily from one position to another as needed.

First position   experiencing something from my own point of view

Second position   experiencing something from the other person's point of view

Third position   experiencing the relationship between 1st and 2nd position from the outside position of a neutral, non-judgmental observer

THINK

What do you think the strengths of each position are? Which position is most useful for teachers? What do you think the problems might be for people who can only operate from one of the positions?

─────────────────── SUGGESTED ANSWERS ───────────────────

* From head on: (A) witch in the mountains, shark in rough seas, one thin witch between two fat ones, road going into infinity, wizard looking at the pyramids, Jaws (B) racing car.
From above: (A) ship going through ice, knife cutting a cake, woman with a long nose and a pointed bra (B) person lifting weights or carrying two loaves of bread.
From below: (A) twig in a bird's beak, Concorde coming into the hangar (B) UFO. And lots more.

Implications

As a teacher, you need to be able to move flexibly from one position to another as appropriate.

First position

- Teach from a position of strength and calm confidence. Make sure you meet your own needs.

- Overstrong: Beware the tendency to be selfish and insensitive to the needs of others.

Second-position

- What is it like to be one of your students? Would you like to be a student in your class?

- Foster a non-judgmental classroom ambience. Help learners feel able to take risks and grow by developing their second-position skills.

- Overstrong: Don't be a doormat. Make sure you give strong enough leadership. Remember, you can't please all the people all the time.

Third position

- Stand back and watch yourself in the classroom. Would you employ you? Are you the teacher you would want to teach your child?

- Make sure you take the time to stand back and look at all the students – and your overall teaching outcomes – objectively from time to time; it's very easy to lose sight of the wood for the trees.

- Overstrong: Be careful you're not seen as too detached and uninvolved, you may seem 'cold'.

Make someone feel good

Getting into rapport through matching or second-positioning someone is one of the basic pillars of NLP which supports many other things. A fundamental, yet often unspoken, guideline of NLP is that in any interaction, you should leave the other person feeling better rather than worse for having crossed your path. Try it. Be nice to someone for no reason. Smile at someone you don't even know. See how it feels.

Here is a story from Jane:

'Why would you want to have people feel better rather than worse?' asked one of the teachers at a summer school in Slovenia, after I had suggested that this might be a nice thing to do. 'Hmm' I thought. 'An interesting question, that tells me quite a bit about the person who asked it!'.

'It's not entirely altruistic,' I replied,' I find that when people feel good around me, I tend to feel good too. I invite you to try it out and discover if it works for you.'

After lunch that day I decided for the first time ever to have a go at swimming across Lake Bled. It isn't a terribly wide lake, but it was certainly quite a challenge for me. And I did it! I swam all the way across and I was delighted. Walking back across the hotel terrace I passed the teacher who had asked the question. 'Been for a swim?' she asked, for it was obvious that I had. 'I've just swum across the lake,' I said, glowing with achievement. 'Really?' she said, 'From where to where?' I explained from where to where.

'Oh,' she said. 'The shortest bit.'

I obviously hadn't got my message across there.

THE META MIRROR

This is a powerful technique for gaining insights into a problematic situation where there is some conflict or difficulty in relating to another person. It enables you to experience a situation from both (or all) points of view and offers the possibility of new understandings which might facilitate change.

You need two chairs, one for you, and one for the other person to whom you want to relate better. If the situation involves more than one person, you can either have a chair for each one, or – especially if large numbers are involved – let one chair represent the whole group. We would, however, suggest that you have just one person in mind the first time.

1 Choose *your* chair and sit in it, being yourself, and looking at the other person whom you imagine to be in the other chair. Tell that person – aloud – how you experience the situation from your point of view.

2 Get up and go and sit in the second chair – *their* chair – and put yourself in their shoes … be them. Look back at yourself sitting in the first chair. Tell the 'you' chair how you experience the situation from this other point of view, using 'I' for them and 'you' for you. Again actually say the words.

3 Stand up, move away from the two chairs and look at both of them and the space between them. Tell them both how you experience the situation now from a neutral observer position.

4 If you are still feeling too involved, even in the observer role, step back once more, and observe the neutral observer observing the two people on the chairs. You are now in 4th position (and you can keep going back as far as you like, if you find it helpful and if it is still giving you useful information).

5 With the insights gained from steps 3 and 4, sit once more in the other person's chair and repeat step 2.

6 Finally sit once more in *your* chair and find out how your experience of the situation is different and whether you have some insights into what you might usefully do to begin to bring about changes.

7 And if you want to do some more experiencing from the different positions, just carry on as long as you need to, but remember to finish off in *your* chair.

Remember to 'break state' each time before taking up a new position. (See page 20)

 TRANSFER TO TEACHING

In class, as well as helping students sort out problems, this activity can be an interesting way of doing role-play or exploiting a dialogue which gives them time to think about the content of the discussion *and* the language to use.

Guided fantasy: Looking from different angles

Sit comfortably in a balanced position. Take a deep breath and as you breathe out, let all the tension drain out of your toes and say to yourself the word RELAX. One more time. Breathe in, let the tension drain away, and RELAX.

Imagine you are holding a rare and beautiful casket that archaeologists have just brought out of an ancient tomb.

Keep the casket closed for the moment and look down on its lid. What can you see? Look at it very carefully. It really is very precious. Handle it gently. Now feel the surface of it with your fingers. Move your fingers slowly over the lid. How does it feel?

You might even like to smell it. Does it have a particular smell?

Look at it from the front. How is it different from the lid? Take a moment to look at it very carefully. Feel the front surface with your fingers. Slowly and carefully. How does that feel?

Look at it and feel it from the side. How is it different from the front? Now the other side. Are both sides the same or are they different?

Turn it around and look at it from behind. Touch it too. What do you notice?

Now, being particularly careful, hold it up to see and feel underneath. What is it like?

Bring the casket down again. In a moment you are going to open it, but before you do, imagine what you will see inside. Imagine it very clearly. And when you're ready, hearing the sound that it makes as you do so, slowly open the lid of the casket ... and ... see whatever you see.

And remember that whatever it is, it too will change as you look at it from different angles.

In a moment, you're going to close the lid and gently come back to the room bringing with you a feeling of wonder and pleasure. When you are ready, open your eyes.

QUIZ – MOTIVATION

What motivates you? Choose one answer for each of the following questions. Put down the first answer you think of. If you think that you wouldn't do either, mark the one you would choose if these were your only options. If both seem true, mark the one you would do first. If you would do different things in different contexts, choose the one you would do most often.

Time limit: 3 minutes

1 What are people more likely to say to you?

  ❑ (a) Act first, think later – that's typical of you!

  ❑ (b) You've talked it to death.
         What are you going to *do* about it?

2 Do you judge your achievements

  ❑ (a) by your own internal standards?
         'I know when I've done a good job.'

  ❑ (b) according to the praise or blame of others?
         'I know how I've done when I see how others react.'

3 Do you prefer

  ❑ (a) to use existing set procedures?

  ❑ (b) to find your own way of doing things?

4 What makes you get on with your work?

  ❑ (a) fear of the consequences of not doing it (the stick)

  ❑ (b) the prospect of reward and success (the carrot)

5 How do you feel about change? Do you prefer

  ❑ (a) things to stay the same, or to evolve over time?

  ❑ (b) lots of variety and change?

6 Do you tend to

  ❑ (a) concentrate on your own behaviour and needs?

  ❑ (b) be strongly influenced by the people around you?

7 Do you work better

  ❑ (a) alone?

  ❑ (b) with others, as part of a team?

8 When you're working, do you prefer

  ❑ (a) to have a clear overview of the task?

  ❑ (b) to think about details and the order of doing things?

Think about your answers as you read the next section on Metaprograms.

Metaprograms: why we do what we do

Just as people perceive the world in different ways, so they react to the world in different ways too. If two people have a job to do, one might plan it carefully, organise the different stages, set specific time limits before starting, and stick to the plan. Another might just start work on those bits which seem the easiest to do, and then see how the job evolves, filling in the gaps as they occur, working right through the night before the deadline. One might do the job totally alone, the other might want a lot of input from other people. This isn't about the quality of the work done at the end – that may or may not be good in either case. It is about the way we prefer to do things and the strategies we use to motivate ourselves.

Some see things as they are and say: 'Why?' I dream things that never were, and say: 'Why not?'

GEORGE BERNARD SHAW

We are bombarded with a huge amount of sensory information all the time and we couldn't possibly take notice of it all. Our brains filter the information we receive and bring to our attention those things which seem to be of importance to us. Have you noticed how you can be totally absorbed in a conversation at a noisy party, and still hear your name spoken in a normal tone of voice across the room? You didn't even know you were listening to that conversation. And you weren't, consciously.

"One man's meat is another man's poison"

TRADITIONAL SAYING

The non-conscious filters our brain habitually uses to select relevant information from our sensory experience are called **'metaprograms'** in NLP*. Once our brain finds a way of behaving that works, it tends to repeat it, so that it becomes a habit, or a 'program'. Metaprograms are some of these basic programs.

Remember:

* different people are motivated by different things and in different ways

* the same person might be motivated in different ways in different contexts

And in case you hadn't thought about it yet, the language you use will affect people's motivation differently. What works for one, won't necessarily work for another. Give information in different ways to motivate all your students.

Implications

♦ Helping your students understand what motivates them individually, might help them to work more productively. It might also help you to organise effective combinations for groupwork.

♦ If you know your preferred behaviour patterns,

you can often make small changes which help you operate more effectively.

♦ If you know what the possible patterns are, you can make sure that you stimulate your students in a variety of different and relevant ways.

---

* Metaprograms in their current form derive from Roger Bailey's Language and Behaviour (LAB) Profile created in the early 1980s, which in turn was based on ideas from NLP developed by Leslie Cameron-Bandler and others. Bailey reduced the original 60 patterns to 14 and developed specific questions to determine each metaprogram. The percentages given throughout this section are from Roger Bailey and apply to the work context in North America, but they may still indicate the bias in the general population in other contexts.

Basic metaprograms

The following are eight of the basic metaprograms. They follow the order of the Motivation quiz on page 120. 1 to 5 are concerned with motivation traits, and 6 to 8 with working traits.

1 Act first or think first

Some people are **proactive:** they act first (sometimes without thinking), they make things happen (15-20%)

Some people are **reactive:** they respond to situations or other people; they often think and plan before they act (15-20%)

Most people are **both:** they initiate action, while being prepared to respond to changing circumstances (60-65%)

You'll probably recognise the students who want to get on with it, and those who want to have all the ground rules clearly sorted out before they commit themselves. This can be a problem if two opposite types are asked to work together on a project. Since most people can work in both modes, it shouldn't be too hard to keep them apart. The following expressions will be helpful for motivating all students – type A for the 'actors', type B for the 'thinkers' and a combination for most people.

A *Do it. Go for it. Get it done. Don't wait.*

B *Think about it carefully. Make sure you really understand.*

2 Internal or external

Some people are **internal:** they evaluate and make judgements for themselves (regardless of what other people think) (40%)

Some people are **external:** they need feedback from others to evaluate things (40%)

Some people are **both:** they use both internal and external feedback (20%)

You are likely to have fairly even numbers of students with an 'internal' or an 'external' metaprogram. In order to cater for both groups, allow room for self-evaluation as well as feedback from you. Get students to check through (and maybe also grade) their own work, and keep a personal estimate and record of their progress which you both can compare with yours.

External feedback can come from other students as well as from you: get weaker and stronger students to collaborate on tasks, and ask students to correct each other's written work.

Where would you place Margaret Thatcher, when she said 'I feel sorry for the other 49'? She was the only one of 50 Commonwealth leaders to oppose sanctions against South Africa during Apartheid.

3 Options or procedures

Some people have an **options** program: they like to have lots of choices about what they do and how they do it (40%)

Some people have a **procedures** program: they like to know the right way to do something, what the correct steps are (40%)

And some people have **both** (20%)

Because of the likelihood of a roughly equal distribution, you need to cater for both types of program. Give rules to learn and steps to follow, and at the same time allow for choice. Make sure you give clear step-by-step instructions for group activities (unless you thrive on chaos), and then offer choices by saying something like: 'OK. I've just described the task, the steps are on the board – you can either work through them as they stand, or you can go about it in your own way. You have 15 minutes.'

Choice can be built in in a variety of other ways: choice between tasks for homework, different groups working on different things, choosing 5 out of 10 questions on a text, choosing 10 words to learn from a list of 30, and so on.

4 Towards or away from

Some people are **towards:** they are motivated by what they want (40%)

Some people are **away from:** they are motivated by what they don't want (40%)

And some people are **both:** usually dependent on context (20%)

Note particularly that it's pretty much a 50/50 split between the two groups, so you really need to consider both types equally.

Which strategy are these people using? Towards (T) or Away From (AF)?

a *My goal is to open a restaurant.*   (   )

b *I don't want to stay on at school.*   (   )

c *Smoking stops me from eating too much.*   (   )

d *I get a kick out of driving fast.*   (   )

Which strategy is this teacher appealing to in each case?

e *This will help you avoid some of the common mistakes people make.*   (   )

f *When you've done this activity, you'll feel much better.*   (   )

Which of the following words would appeal to which strategy type?

g *attain, get, achieve, obtain*   (   )

h *avoid, steer clear of, get rid of*   (   )*

─────────────── SUGGESTED ANSWERS ───────────────

* a=T (Towards) b=AF (Away From) c=AF d=T e=AF f=T g=T h=AF

5 Sameness or difference

A few people have a strong **sameness** program: they notice what is the same about things and they tend to like stability (5%)

Most people have a **sameness with exception** program: they notice what is the same about things and the exceptions, and they like a certain amount of stability with the occasional change (65%)

Some people have a **difference** program: they notice what is different about things, and they love change (20%)

And yet other people have a **sameness with exception and difference** program: they like both evolution and revolution (10%)

You need to combine a certain amount of routine (sameness) with some variety (difference) in order to satisfy most of the people most of the time.

'Sameness' people will be helped if we make links between new teaching and something familiar, eg by saying: 'This is like X that we did last term'.

People with a 'difference' program will be helped if you say something like: 'This is completely new and it isn't like anything you've ever done before'.

As a teacher or trainer, you need to be able to use 'sameness' language and 'difference' language simultaneously. How? You say something like: 'This is completely new but it's a bit like X!'

Some sameness language: *like, same, identical, similar, familiar, connects, reminds (of)…*

Some difference language: *new, different, not like, unlike, unique, special, original …*

6 Attention direction

Most people are aware of **others:** they respond to the people around them (93%)

A few are absorbed in **self:** they are oblivious to the people around them (7%)

Most people operate more effectively and learn better when they feel good about those around them and when the people around them feel good. That's what this book is about – being aware of others, responding flexibly, making others feel good.

The rare people who are totally self-absorbed will often focus well on the task at hand – as long as there's a clear pay-off for them.

7 Style

Some people like to be very **independent:** they prefer working alone without interruption and they like taking control and responsibility (20%)

Some are **co-operative:** they like sharing responsibility as part of a team (20%)

Most people are **both:** they like being in charge without the responsibility of standing alone, so they need to work with and be supported by others (60%)

The traditional classroom, with students working alone, only suits about a fifth of students. Most people learn better working in groups, and they benefit from being a group leader sometimes. Give the loners time to work – and shine – alone.

8 General or specific

Do you see the wood or the trees?

Most people are **general:** they like to have the big picture (60%)

A few people are **specific:** they like to focus on the details (15%)

And some people are **both:** they like to have the big picture and the details (25%)

- Give an overview of the work you are going to do with students at the beginning of the year, term, week and lesson.

- Give students time at the end of a session to process the detail and note down a summary or an overview. A 'wordstorm' satisfies both the general and the specific types. (See page 24)

- Simplified children's books often give an enjoyable and easily accessible overview of a new subject for study. Skimming through a simplified reader before you look in detail at a literary classic can be particularly helpful – like seeing the picture on the box before you start a jigsaw puzzle.

> If you want to know more about the fascinating area of metaprograms, read Shelle Rose Charvet's excellent book 'Words that Change Minds'

 STRATEGIES

Make a list of ten things you have to do regularly which you are reluctant to do, which you don't really enjoy doing, or which you sometimes have problems getting started, eg the ironing, writing letters, marking homework, putting up shelves, getting out of bed in the morning …

You do these things, so presumably you have strategies which make you do them (eventually). What strategies do you use? Write down exactly what it is that finally makes you do the task.

Susan's notes for getting out of bed are: set the alarm clock ten minutes earlier than I need to get up; when I first wake up, mentally review the day ahead and any specific tasks I need to do or times when I need to do them; then revise my getting up time to the very last minute necessary in order to achieve the first objective. Of course this can all be upset by having to get up immediately to answer the phone!

Look back through the list of metaprograms and compare them with your notes.

Can you add to your notes to have a fuller understanding of how you operate?

Can you see better strategies than some of the ones you are currently using?

 TRANSFER TO TEACHING

Doing this activity in pairs or small groups provides excellent practice of the present simple and giving advice (Why don't you …?)

 KIM'S GAME

Write down from memory the eight metaprograms described in this section.

Verb power

From noun to verb

The parts of speech we use can affect how we experience things. A nominalisation is the result when a process has been fossilised into an abstract noun. Nouns are somewhat fixed. We learned in school that a noun is a 'person, place or thing'. You don't change people, places and things. They exist. They are there. Which is fine for concrete nouns.

Unfortunately abstract nouns such as 'love', 'relationships', 'respect' and 'happiness' are quite clearly transitory and changing when we look at them objectively, but when we are emotionally involved we forget objectivity and we begin to view these abstractions as if they really exist and as if they are as fixed as other nouns.

How can you tell if it's a concrete noun (which can't easily be changed), or an abstract noun (which can)? If you can't put it in a container, then it's abstract.

Verbs, on the other hand, are much more fluid. We do things, and this implies movement, process and change. So, if we (or other people) are getting stuck in 'relationships' which aren't going anywhere, or are having problems with 'behaviour' or 'management', you can reintroduce the idea of a possible change by turning a noun into a verb.

Which do you think are the key words in these three examples?*

1 *I've got a terrible relationship with my colleague.*

   How could you relate differently, do you think?

2 *He's useless at management.*

   Could you do something to help him manage better?

3 *I don't get any respect around here.*

   What do you see people doing when they are respecting you?

What might you say to help these people think differently about their problems?

4 *I'm hopeless at organisation.*

5 *Success is so elusive!*

6 *I just don't seem to have the knowledge.*

7 *I'm only asking for a bit more freedom!*

8 *I'm such a bloody failure!*

--------- SUGGESTED ANSWERS ---------

* (1) relationship/relate (2) management/manage (3) respect/are respecting (4) What would it take to be able to organise things well? (5) In what ways do you want to succeed? (6) What exactly is it that you don't know? and What *do* you know in relation to that? (7) How do you want to be free? Give me some examples of being free. What could you do that would free you up? (8) In what ways are you failing specifically? and What are the ways in which you are succeeding?

From past to present ... and present to past

You may be surprised to know that tenses are influential too – all the more so if we reframe them and call them ... *relaxes!*

The verb forms we use to describe our experience (a) give it a time reference – present, past, future – and (b) indicate whether it is more or less likely – by means of conditionals or modals. If, for example, you put a lot of your strengths and qualities into the past, eg *'I used to be so energetic'*, you might try bringing them into the present for a change, ending up with a sort of positive affirmation: *'I'm so energetic!'*. If you've done it once, you can do it again. (Won't you?)

On the other hand, if someone says *'I'm going through a terrible time'*, the use of the present continuous tense means it is still very much part of their current experience, and it is probably very hard for them to envisage anything beyond it. A possible challenge to this might be to say: *'Tell me about this terrible time you've been going through ...'* The use of the present perfect continuous tense slips their terrible time at least partly into the past, and makes it less present. It allows them to begin to move away from their problems, freeing them to focus on possible solutions.

The English present perfect tense is very useful here because of its links with both the past and the present. It enables us to acknowledge another person's present experience and move it into the past at the same time. Using the past tense *'Tell me about this terrible time you went through ...'* is much less subtle and less respectful, as well as sounding somewhat odd. By completely disregarding their present experience, we risk totally breaking rapport.

If your native language does not have a direct equivalent of the English present perfect tense, think of ways in which you can express simultaneous ideas of past and present, or otherwise help a person move beyond a particular problem?

You might say something like *'That sounded really terrible.'* By putting their telling of the story (about the terrible event) into the past, you add the possibility of putting the event itself into the past.

What could you say to these people? (Consider the Precision Model too on page 66)

1 *I'm feeling really negative about everything.*

2 *My son is being so difficult at the moment.*

3 *You're such a stubborn person!*

4 *I'm finding it so difficult to remember all these irregular verbs.*

5 *I'm so confused about conditionals!**

––––––––––––––––––– SUGGESTED ANSWERS –––––––––––––––––––

* (1) What have you been feeling negative about particularly? (2) How has he been difficult? (3) I admit I have been a bit stubborn ... (4) Which ones in particular have you been finding it difficult to remember? (5) What exactly have you been confused about?

The meaning of my communication is the response I get

This presupposition is about taking responsibility for my actions and for my life. Do I make things happen? Or do I let things happen? Either way, I have always had a choice about what I have done, and I have a choice about what I do next. The message is: I am responsible for what happens when I say or do something.

"I asked for that!"

If I don't like the response I am getting from someone, then I need to do something different to get a different response. It may well be true that another person or other people are partly to blame for whatever is happening, but moaning and blaming other people – however comforting that might be – isn't going to change anything. If I want change, I have to initiate it myself.

OK. We know that this doesn't always work. There are times with some people, when whatever you do and however much you try, you will not get the resolution you want. Some people just don't like me (hard though that may be to understand), and maybe I'm not prepared to do anything and everything necessary to make them like me. There are certain beliefs I won't compromise on. That's my choice. If you have this NLP presupposition in mind, however, you are much more likely to have successful relationships with people. At least try a few different approaches before giving up.

If 'responsibility' were spelt 'respons-Ability', (meaning 'the ability to respond'), how would you feel differently about it?

And of course we know that you cannot control your life totally. You cannot control everything that happens to other people – that would be taking away their choice. You cannot control the weather and other natural phenomena. Life can throw things at you that are not of your choosing. What you can choose, however, is how you respond to those things. We are all part of a system; we are influenced by the system and in turn we influence it ourselves.

Implications

- If the students don't seem to be learning what you seem to be teaching, don't assume it's their fault. Try another approach.

- If you're getting a negative reaction from one, some or all of your students, find out what the problem is and do something different.

- Help students take responsibility for their own learning. Incorporate 'learning to learn' strategies and self-evaluation into your lessons.

- Encourage students to take initiatives.

CHANGE YOUR RESPONSE

1 Think of a person with whom you have some kind of conflict and who you would like to relate to better. Even if you know the conflict is their fault. (Especially if you know it's their fault.) Start with a simple relationship, like the one you have with a shopkeeper.

2 Write down all the things that you might be doing to exacerbate the situation. Yes, go on! Be honest! You don't have to tell anyone else. (Even if it's definitely the other person's fault, just note how you're not helping.)

3 Now write down at least three things you might do differently which might improve the situation.

> Try to present at least three options. One is no choice at all. Two creates a dilemma. With three you begin to have real choice and flexibility.

4 Try your strategies out with the person. One by one, or all together. Enjoy your new relationship.

5 Try it with someone else.

THINK AGAIN!

1 Remember a lesson you taught or a training-session you gave that didn't go as well as you would have liked it to.

2 Make a list of three things that you could have done differently – and note them on your lesson / session plan.

3 Try out those things the next time you do the same lesson or session.

4 Get used to doing this regularly with every lesson you give. Watch your teaching improve dramatically!

Jane was staying at a conference centre when the woman in the room above her started making a regular thumping noise which went on and on and on. It was after midnight (and it wasn't that sort of thumping noise), so she went upstairs, tapped on the door and politely explained that she couldn't sleep and asked the woman if she would mind being a little bit quieter. The woman said she was killing cockroaches. Jane raised an eyebrow in disbelief, but went back to bed. And the noise started up again.

> *"If what you're doing isn't working, try something else!"*
>
> **NLP** ADAGE

Jane stood on the desk, thumped hard on the ceiling with her shoe and yelled 'JUST SHUT UP!'

The noise stopped immediately – and didn't start again.

A different strategy. And it worked!

 WHAT DID YOU
REALLY MEAN?

1 Think of the last time someone reacted badly to something you said.

a) What was the person's frame of mind and focus of attention before you spoke?

b) What words did you say?

c) What tone of voice did you use?

d) What was your posture?

e) What gestures did you use?

f) What were you really saying to them?

Overall, what was the message you were sending to them? Were you actually trying to pick a fight? Were you defending yourself from their expected criticism in advance? Were you being critical of them? Was there something about them that you didn't like or approve of that they picked up on?

2 Now state precisely the outcome you wanted. Assuming that you didn't want to pick a fight, what exactly did you want? A change in behaviour? The washing up done? A friendly chat? What? (If you were trying to pick a fight, is there anything else you could more productively have been doing?)

3 How could you have got across your message in 2 more successfully? Rephrase and answer the questions a-f, like this:

a) *What's the best time for me to talk to this person from their point of view?*

b) *What words should I use?*

and so on.

 TRANSFER TO TEACHING

All the activities in this section can profitably be used with students simply by making the content relevant. When students have identified examples of communication which has gone awry and/or communication strategies they already use, ask them to work in small groups and improvise or roleplay the conversations. The group then think of alternative ways of handling the conversation. They replay the scene as many times as necessary, improving both their use of language and strategies, until they are satisfied with the outcome.

 THINK

Do you agree or disagree with the following sayings?

What we say is what we mean

There's many a true word spoken in jest

Modelling: the study of excellence

'Good teachers are born, not made.' True or false?

Some people are born teachers. They seem naturally to inspire others to learn. Others of us have to work a bit harder, but the NLP view is that good teachers can be made, or rather they can *make themselves*. Assuming obvious physical and mental provisos, if someone can do something, then I can learn to do it too, by 'modelling' myself on that person. For, according to another NLP presupposition, *modelling excellent behaviour leads to excellence.*

At various times in their lives, people often take others as role models, whether consciously or non-consciously. Most of us started teaching in the way that we ourselves were taught. Even if we didn't find it particularly inspiring, we thought that's what teaching was.

> *"People seldom improve when they have no other model but themselves to copy."*
>
> **GOLDSMITH**

Modelling was the starting point for the whole system of beliefs and techniques that make up NLP. Find someone who can do something extremely well, find out exactly what it is they do, and if you do exactly what they do, you too will be excellent. The word 'exactly' is important here. Full modelling involves observing external behaviour as well as finding out (somehow) the internal mental processes. What are their values and beliefs? How does the person think? What are their strategies or metaprograms? (See page121) What precise sequence of precise submodalities is involved in their internal representations? (See page 73) How much do they eat, drink, exercise? How often do they practise? Which of the things they do are the ones which make a difference to the actual skill you want to acquire? Can you acquire just that skill without replicating the person's life in all other respects? Until you can isolate *the difference that makes the difference,* you need to model it all.

So the bad news is that modelling is no small thing. The good news is that people learn and improve by 'copying' others. Not everyone wants to win the Olympics or be the best in the world at something. You can start small. You can start now.

Implications

- If there's something you want to be good at, model someone who is good at it. And if there's something you want to be better at, then model someone who is better at it than you!

- If you want to be an excellent teacher, model excellent teachers. Look at what they do, how they act, what sort of relationship they have with their students and colleagues. Ask them how they feel about what they do. What are their beliefs? Second position them. (See page 116) Imagine what it's like to be them. As you learn techniques and strategies, start putting them into practice.

- Share modelling strategies with students. Set the project of modelling good learners. Encourage them to share and try out strategies they learn.

- If you want to speak a language like a native speaker, model native speakers.

- If you want your students to be a grade A students, you know how to help them!

 JANE'S COURAGE
BOOSTER!

1 Imagine a crunchy situation you're a bit nervous about. For example, going to the dentist, a job interview, preparing dinner for 20 people, a date with a new person in your life …

2 See yourself doing the activity or being in the situation as though you are watching a video in your mind. (The video is about 20 x 15 cms, about 20 cms away from you, slightly above your head and slightly to the right.) Watch it through from the beginning, and notice each step of the way, each thing you will do, culminating in the successful completion of your 'ordeal'. It is important that you see yourself having completed everything successfully. Enjoy the feeling of success. Congratulate yourself 'Well done!'

3 Do 2 again, and fast forward the video to the end. Wallow in the success. And then do it again.

4 Next hear your internal voice giving you encouragement, saying, for example 'Go for it. You can do it'. Use whatever words seem right for you.

5 Now you're ready to do whatever it is. If you can, rehearse the situation by yourself in front of a mirror, and/or with someone else for support. Then rehearse again just before the real thing. And enjoy your success!

In brief:

1 Think of a challenging situation   3 Encourage yourself

2 Rehearse it visually   4 Do it!

In long:

If you really want to go for it, try the 'simple' modelling strategy on the next page.

 SHARE YOUR
BAD HABITS

If you want to kill two birds with one stone and experience what is involved in modelling while getting rid of a bad habit, try teaching that bad habit to someone else. Explain in absolute detail what it is you do, when, why, what's going on inside your head. What pictures are you making? What sounds and voices are you hearing? What sub-modalities are involved and in what order?

You can either do this with another person, who might be asking questions as you explain, or you can write down precise instructions.

When you think you have explained clearly, go back and fill in additional details. Imagine your life depends on them being able to take your place and carry out this bad habit exactly for you while you're away.

When you look at the complex behaviour pattern you run through in order to carry out this bad habit, can you think of any short-cuts or ways of interrupting or diverting the pattern so that you do something more profitable instead?

A SIMPLE
MODELLING STRATEGY

1   First have a well-formed **outcome** in relation to a skill you would like to have or improve. (See page 59) If you are nervous of public speaking, for example, your outcome might be to deliver a speech to a particular group or people, speaking confidently and clearly in an entertaining way.

2   Find two or three **models,** people who have the skill you want to have – preferably people you know and can talk to, although you might also watch confident public speakers on TV, or read about public speakers. One person will do, but finding several people means you're more likely to identify key elements of the strategy used.

"The quality of a person's life is in direct proportion to their commitment to excellence, regardless of their chosen field of endeavour."

VINCE LOMBARDI

3   **Observe** what they do externally (if this is possible) and try it out yourself. This is all the more effective if you second-position them and imagine what it's like to be them as you do the activity. (See page 116)

4   Interview your models to find out what's going on internally. You will probably discover a combination of certain **beliefs** that they have about themselves (eg 'I know I can do it') and a **strategy,** ie a sequence of representations in a particular order. Find out the **submodalities** involved in any representation that is part of their strategy sequence, so you can do exactly the same thing in the same way (and in the same order). Ask the sorts of questions you practised in the section on **submodalities** (See page 73) and look at the sorts of things to ask about in the section on **metaprograms** (See page 121)

5   Next, try out the strategy to see if it works for you. Your model has almost certainly practised in order to reach the level of skill you are aspiring to, so you too need to put in the practice. If it works, great! If it doesn't, go back over the steps to find out if there's anything you've missed, maybe a key belief or a representation or a crucial submodality, and incorporate the missing piece. Then practise some more before testing the strategy again.

Does that seem like a lengthy endeavour? It is. (And this is the simplified version!) But just think of the potential rewards of improving old skills and learning new ones – and in such an interesting way! Remember that it is not enough just to understand what someone else is doing, you need to *do it*. And practise!

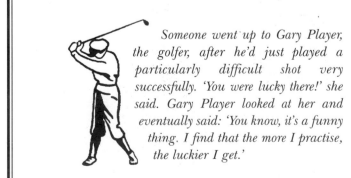

Someone went up to Gary Player, the golfer, after he'd just played a particularly difficult shot very successfully. 'You were lucky there!' she said. Gary Player looked at her and eventually said: 'You know, it's a funny thing. I find that the more I practise, the luckier I get.'

Modelling: the bare essentials

When Jane did her NLP Master Practitioner modelling project, she modelled people who swim outdoors throughout the winter in a natural lake, sometimes breaking the ice to get into the water. Her 'courage booster' was the basic strategy that she developed for getting into cold water. The wonderful thing about it is that she can now use it in lots of other challenging situations – going to the dentist or before giving a talk to a large audience.

The difference between ordinary and extraordinary is that little extra.

Susan has always been ultra-pathetic about getting into 'cold' water; even a swimming pool in Spain in the summer could take ten minutes. But one morning she decided to go with Jane to the lake and do a simplified modelling strategy based on what she could observe and what she knew of Jane and herself.

♦ She visualised success and how good she would feel afterwards.

♦ Copying Jane, she walked three steps down into the water (up to her knees), and turned round and looked at the lake. She adjusted the strap of her costume (– not sure if this was an essential part of the strategy, but you never know), went down the next three steps, turned round and without hesitation started swimming. Mentally she added the words they had said at the firewalk, 'Cool moss' – which seemed fitting and more believable than 'warm bath' – she'd tried that one before without success.

♦ She knew instantly that she'd made a terrible mistake and that she was about to die, but she decided to die heroically and swam three more strokes. And then the magic happened. It didn't feel quite so bad. They swam twice round the lake.

Susan's only been once more to the lake. That isn't really the point. She knows she can do it if she wants to. The point is that it's transformed all her other swimming experiences. Getting into swimming pools is fun!

The Wise Teacher and the Jar

here was once a very wise teacher, whose words of wisdom students would come from far and wide to hear. One day as usual, many students began to gather in the teaching room. They came in and sat down very quietly, looking to the front with keen anticipation, ready to hear what the teacher had to say.

Eventually the teacher came in and sat down in front of the students. The room was so quiet you could hear a pin drop. On one side of the teacher was a large glass jar. On the other side was a pile of dark grey rocks. Without saying a word, the teacher began to pick up the rocks one by one and place them very carefully in the glass jar. (Plonk. Plonk.) When all the rocks were in the jar, the teacher turned to the students and asked, 'Is the jar full?' 'Yes,' said the students. 'Yes, teacher, the jar is full.'

Without saying a word, the teacher began to drop small round pink pebbles carefully into the large glass jar so that they fell down between the rocks. (Clickety click. Clickety click.) When all the pebbles were in the jar, the teacher turned to the students and asked, 'Is the jar now full?' The students looked at one another and then some of them started nodding and saying, 'Yes. Yes, teacher, the jar is now full. Yes.'

Without saying a word, the teacher took some fine silver sand and let it trickle with a gentle sighing sound into the large glass jar (whoosh) where it settled around the pink pebbles and the dark grey rocks. When all the sand was in the jar, the teacher turned to the students and asked, 'Is the jar now full?'

The students were not so confident this time, but the sand had clearly filled all the space in the jar, so a few still nodded and said, 'Yes, teacher, the jar is now full. Now it's full.'

Without saying a word, the teacher took a jug of water and poured it carefully, without splashing a drop, into the large glass jar. (Gloog. Gloog.) When the water reached the brim, the teacher turned to the students and asked, 'Is the jar now full?' Most of the students were silent, but two or three ventured to answer, 'Yes, teacher, the jar is now full. Now it is.'

Without saying a word, the teacher took a handful of salt and sprinkled it slowly over the top of the water with a very quiet whishing sound. (Whish.) When all the salt had dissolved into the water, the teacher turned to the students and asked once more, 'Is the jar now full?' The students were totally silent. Eventually one brave student said, 'Yes, teacher. The jar is now full.' 'Yes,' said the teacher. 'The jar is now full.'

The teacher then said, 'A story always has many meanings and you will each have understood many things from this demonstration. Discuss quietly amongst yourselves what meanings the story has for you. How many different messages can you find in it and take from it?'

The students looked at the wise teacher and at the beautiful glass jar filled with grey rocks, pink pebbles, silver sand, water and salt. Then they quietly discussed with one another the meanings the story had for them. After a few minutes the wise teacher raised one hand and the room fell silent. The teacher said, 'Remember that there is never just one interpretation of anything. You have all taken away many meanings and messages from the story, and each meaning is as important and as valid as any other.'

And without saying another word, the teacher got up and left the room.

Flexibility

The fourth pillar of NLP and perhaps the most crucial part of the Basic Action Model, flexibility is what NLP is all about. It's what this book is all about. It's about giving you more choices.

A final story from Jane

On one occasion I was telling the story about the butterfly in your hands to a group of teachers, students and directors in central London. I paused dramatically, as I always do, just after the sister had asked her question, to give the group a chance to anticipate the old man's answer. It was a beautiful, hushed, expectant moment. It was very quickly broken, by a question from a lady in the front row. 'Would the girls have spoken in those voices?' she asked. Hiding my surprise at the question (and my annoyance at the interruption), I said that as the girls were very young, they probably had higher voices than the ones I gave them. I really didn't know. What I did know, however, was that I could probably expect more such challenging questions from that particular source!

Sure enough, later on in the session, I was talking about the NLP presupposition that body and mind are interconnected. I had just said that if you are in a negative state of mind and you want to change to a more positive one, one of the things you might try for a start, is to change your downward, negative physiology to a more upward, positive one: straighten up, look up, breathe more deeply and so on. I was about to carry on, when there came another question from the lady in the front row: 'What if someone has died?'

I was slightly stunned by this, and it took me a moment to understand what she meant. Then I realised what a wonderful question it was.

I think NLP puts some people off because there seems to be a kind of Mary Poppinsyness about it: that you have to go round being nice and jolly and happy all the time. What this lady was asking was: 'Isn't it OK to grieve?' And by implication, 'Isn't it OK to feel 'negative': sad, angry, frustrated, depressed... ?' She was asking: 'Do we have to be in a good, positive state all the time?'

Well the answer is no, of course we don't. It's appropriate and it's healing to grieve or feel angry or whatever, because those feelings help us ... for a time. But equally, there comes a time when grief or anger are no longer useful, either for us or for the people around us. And it's at that moment – if we want to – that it's helpful to be able to choose to change our state. Choose to do something different.

NLP is about having more choices in your life.

You can choose to stay as you are.

Or you can choose to move on.

Or you can choose to do a bit of both.

What is important is to have the choice.

It's ... in your hands.

Our deepest fear is not that we are inadequate.

*Our deepest fear is that
we are powerful beyond measure.*

*It is our light, not our darkness,
that most frightens us.*

*We ask ourselves: Who am I to be brilliant,
gorgeous, talented and fabulous?*

Actually, who are you not to be?

You are a child of the universe.

Your playing small doesn't serve the world.

*There is nothing enlightening about shrinking
so that other people won't feel insecure around you.*

*We are born to make manifest
the glory of the universe that is within us.*

It is not just in some of us: it is in everyone.

*And as we let our own light shine,
we unconsciously give other people
permission to do the same.*

*And as we are liberated from our own fear,
our presence automatically liberates others.*

MARIANNE WILLIAMSON: A RETURN TO LOVE

Teaching suggestions

We recommended in the introduction that you consider offering to students the ideas about NLP that we present in this book. Throughout the book we have also given suggestions for way of making some of the activities relevant to language students. Here we suggest ways of exploiting other specific parts of the book.

Stories

The stories were designed to be heard, either read aloud by the teacher or listened to on the accompanying cassette. You can also coach students to tell them as an enjoyable way of working on pronunciation. Concentrate specifically on elision, stress, intonation and emphasis to express meaning. Encourage students to speak slowly and clearly while making eye contact with the audience so that they can easily be understood. The stories can also be presented as reading passages. However, please remember two guiding principles:

- **Stories are above all for enjoyment.** As teachers of English we want to exploit them for language purposes, but we must take care not to milk them dry and kill the joy. Just exploit stories enough for students to be enriched by them.

- **Stories have many meanings.** *The map is not the territory.* Different people may interpret the stories in different ways. Allow for individual interpretations even if they do not coincide with your own. (Some of our meanings can be guessed by reading the section immediately before each story in the book.)

You might also bear in mind that metaphor works at a non-conscious level. Sometimes you may want to leave the story open without discussing its meanings, so that students can go on processing both consciously and non-consciously.

Did your students understand how the punchline of the first story in this book is held over to the title page, to make the reader think what the old man might have said?

Here are some suggestions for exploiting the stories.

- Tell part of the story up to a suitably dramatic moment and then ask students to think what might happen next. Or simply leave them to ponder until you finish the story later. This is particularly effective with 'In Your Hands', 'The Drought', and 'Sir Gawain and the Loathley Lady'. Accept all suggestions students make, without confirming or denying them. They will be able to compare their own ideas with the original when they hear the end of the story. They might even prefer their own version and their own message.

- Invite students to join in with the telling of the story. This works well with repeated lines, such as 'Please. please don't throw me into that bramble patch' (Brer Rabbit), and 'Is the jar now full?' (The Wise Teacher and the Jar). And with 'The Drought' you can invite them to suggest other groups of people (or other creatures) who went into the temple, before you get to the bit about the little girl: 'So another day all the _____ went into the temple to pray for rain.'

- Ask students to close their eyes and feel themselves inside the story. How hot and thirsty can they feel in 'The Drought'? Can they really experience Asclepius' lunch? Are their mouths watering as they see it, feel it, smell it, taste it and hear themselves biting into it?

Relaxation

The more you practise doing guided visualisation and relaxation, the easier it gets. Use the basic relaxation (see page 22) on a regular basis, either as preparation for guided fantasies or in lessons to help students to concentrate. Once they are used to it, it can be a great help at times of stress, such as examinations.

Guided fantasies

Read the text first. With guided fantasies, it is important that students understand the text before they start or they may become distracted and find it difficult to let their minds wander. Let students read the text first and deal with any difficulties they may have. Then they can put the text aside and really get into the fantasy.

Get students comfortable before they listen. Before you begin any fantasy, ask students to make themselves comfortable and symmetrical, ie no crossed arms or legs, in a position they can easily maintain for several minutes without moving too much. Tell them that they will be asked to close their eyes. They don't have to do so, but they will probably find it easier to imagine things with their eyes closed. Pre-teach the words 'breathe' and 'swallow' and tell them to do both as necessary.

Get feedback afterwards ... if appropriate. Some fantasies are quite general and students may be happy to share what they have imagined – possibly after having drawn a representation or doodle of it first. Other fantasies can be very personal, in which case we should respect the students' privacy. As to feedback on the language, the students may be very receptive to the language while they are relaxed, but it is usually more suitable to check their understanding at another time.

Quotations

Copy the larger quotations onto coloured card and display them on the walls as additional sensory stimulus. With the smaller quotations, you can write a different one on the board each day. This acts as an excellent focus for discussion until the whole group is assembled. The quotations can also lead to more formal debate.

● ●

———————————— SUGGESTED ANSWERS TO TASKS ON PAGE 33 ————————————

Can/can't Present the basic structure on board. Have a questionnaire for students to fill in, asking one another what they can and can't do. They report back to the class and/or write up their results.
Mistakes Teacher says/writes on board sentences containing mistakes. Students stand up when they know what the mistakes are. Those who are standing reach a consensus on the mistakes and then quietly tell sitting students until everyone is standing up. Volunteers write correct versions on board.
Dialogue Students have half the dialogue each and dictate it to one another. They then mime their side of the dialogue to their partner, possibly while saying the 'tune' of the words to 'la', eg *'Hello. How are you?'* becomes *'la-la. la-LA-la?'*. Students stand at opposite sides of the room and say their parts with maximum emphasis to a partner opposite, who repeats it back to them, copying the exaggerated emphasis before saying their own part for their partner to copy likewise.
Letter Students collaborate on the content of the letter but can only communicate through mime or pictures. Individually they then write a version of the letter and read it aloud to the others. The group then collaborates orally (without looking at any written version other than their own) to create the best joint version which everyone writes down. They check each other's copy for layout, spelling, etc.
Story telling See previous page.

Booklist

NLP – basic

Richard BANDLER *Using your brain for a change* [Real People Press] 1985

Tad JAMES *The Secret of Creating your Future* [Advanced Neuro Dynamics] 1989

Genie LABORDE *Influencing with Integrity* [Syntony Publishing] 1987

Genie LABORDE *90 Days to Communication Excellence* [Syntony Publishing] 1985

Joseph O'CONNOR & Ian MCDERMOTT *Principles of NLP*
        [Thorsons-HarperCollins] 1996

Anthony ROBBINS *Notes from a Friend* [Fireside] 1995

NLP – more advanced

Dr Harry ALDER *NLP the New Art & Science of Getting What you Want* [Piatkus] 1994

Connirae ANDREAS & Steve ANDREAS *Heart of the Mind* [Real People Press] 1989

Steve & Connirae ANDREAS *Change your Mind and Keep the Change*
        [Real People Press] 1987

Steve ANDREAS & Charles FAULKNER *NLP the New Technology of Achievement*
        [Quill, William Morrow] 1994

Richard BANDLER *Magic in Action* [Meta Publications] 1992

Richard BANDLER & John GRINDER *Frogs into Princes* [Real People Press] 1979

Richard BANDLER & John GRINDER *ReFraming: NLP and the Transformation of
        Meaning* [Real People Press] 1982

Richard BANDLER & John GRINDER *The Structure of Magic* [Science & Behaviour
        Books] 1979

Shelle Rose CHARVET *Words that Change Minds* [Kendall/Hunt]

Sue KNIGHT *NLP at Work* [Nicholas Brealey] 1995

Joseph O'CONNOR & John SEYMOUR *Introducing NLP*
        [Thorsons-Harper Collins] 1993

Joseph O'CONNOR & John SEYMOUR *Training with NLP* [Thorsons] 1994

Teaching and learning

Jill ANDERSON *Thinking, Changing, Rearranging* [Metamorphous Press] 1981

Diana BEAVER *Lazy Learning* [Element] 1994

Diana BEAVER *Easy Being* [Useful Book Company] 1997

Michele & Craig BORBA *Self-esteem, a Classroom Affair,* Vols 1&2
        [Harper & Row] 1978 & 1982

Donna BRANDES & Paul GINNIS *A Guide to Student-Centred Learning*
        [Basil Blackwell] 1986

Bernard CLEVELAND *Master Teaching Techniques*
        [The Connecting Link Press] 1986

Paul and Gail DENNISON *Brain Gym* [Edu-Kinesthetics Inc] 1986

Robert DILTS and Todd EPSTEIN *Dynamic Learning* [Meta Publications] 1995

Michael J GELB & Tony BUZAN *Lessons from the Art of Juggling*
        [Crown Trade Paperbacks] 1994

Fred Noah GORDON *Magical Classroom* [Zephyr Press] 1995

Michael GRINDER *Righting the Educational Conveyor Belt*
        [Metamorphous Press] 1991

Carla HANNAFORD *Smart Moves* [Great Ocean Publishers] 1995

Eric JENSEN *The Learning Brain* [Turning Point] 1994

Eric JENSEN *Super Teaching* [Turning Point] 1995

Eric JENSEN *Brain-Based Learning* [Turning Point] 1996

Eric JENSEN *Completing the Puzzle* [Turning Point] 1996

Eric JENSEN *Brain Compatible Strategies* [Turning Point] 1997

Peter KLINE *The Everyday Genius* [Great Ocean Publishers] 1988

Michael LAWLOR *Inner Track Learning* [Pilgrims] 1988

Linda LLOYD *Classroom Magic* [Metamorphous Press] 1990

Barbara MEISTER VITALE *Unicorns are Real* [Warner Books] 1986

Colin ROSE *Accelerated Learning* [Accelerated Learning Systems] 1985

Paul SCHEELE *Natural Brilliance* [Learning Strategies Corporation] 1997

Alistair SMITH *Accelerated Learning in the Classroom*
       [Network Educational Press] 1996

Enhancing ability

Dr Brian M ALMAN & Dr Peter LAMBROU *Self-Hypnosis* [Souvenir Press] 1983

Tony BUZAN *Use Your Head* [BBC] 1974

Tony BUZAN *The Mind Map Book* [BBC] 1993

Tony BUZAN & Raymond KEENE *Book of Genius* [Stanley Paul] 1994

Leslie CAMERON-BANDLER, David GORDON & Michael LEBEAU *Know How*
       [Real People Press] 1985

Stephen COVEY *The Seven Habits of Highly Effective People* [Simon & Schuster] 1992

Bobbi DE PORTER *Quantum Learning* [Piatkus] 1992

Robert DILTS, Tim HALLBOM & Suzi SMITH *Beliefs (Pathways to Health and
       Well-Being)* [Metamorphous Press] 1990

Betty EDWARDS *Drawing on the Right Side of the Brain*
       [Jeremy P Tarcher/Perigee Books] 1989

Daniel GOLEMAN *Emotional Intelligence* [Bloomsbury] 1996

Daniel GOLEMAN *Vital Lies, Simple Truths* [Bloomsbury] 1997

Louise L HAY *You Can Heal Your Life* [Eden Grove] 1984

Robert HOLDEN *Laughter The Best Medicine* [Thorsons] 1993

Robert HOLDEN *Living Wonderfully* [Thorsons] 1994

Robert HOLDEN *Stress Busters* [Thorsons] 1992

Susan JEFFERS *Feel the Fear and Do it Anyway* [Arrow] 1991

Henriette Anne KLAUSER *Writing on Both Sides of the Brain*
       [Harper San Francisco] 1987

Patrick K PORTER *Awaken the Genius* [Purelight Publishing] 1993

Denis POSTLE *The Mind Gymnasium* [Macmillan] 1989

Marilyn VOS SAVANT & Leonore FLEISCHER *Brain Power* [Piatkus] 1990

Virginia SATIR *Making Contact* [Celestial Arts] 1976

Anthony ROBBINS *Unlimited Power* [Simon & Schuster] 1988

Tom WUJEC *The Complete Mental Fitness Book* [Aurum Press] 1989

Marilee ZDENEK *The Right-Brain Experience* [Corgi] 1983

Useful addresses

ANLP
(The Association for Neuro-Linguistic
Programming)
PO Box 10
Porthmadog
WALES
LL48 6ZB
Tel +44 (0)870 870 4970
Fax +44 (0)870 165 6231
Web www.anlp.org
Publishers of RAPPORT, the quarterly
ANLP magazine

INLPTA
(The International NLP Trainers
Association)
PO Box 288
Fareham
Hants
PO16 0YG
Tel +44 (0)1329 285353
Fax +44 (0)1329 285757
Email inlpta@aol.com
Web http://members.aol.com/inlpta/index.htm

IATEFL
(The International Association for
Teachers of English as a Foreign
Language)
3 Kingsdown Chambers
Kingsdown Park
Whitstable
Kent
CT5 2FL
Tel +44 (0)1227 276528
Fax +44 (0)1227 274415
Email iatefl@compuserve.com
Web www.iatefl.org

SEAL
(The Society for Effective Affective
Learning)
Directors
37 Park Hall Road
East Finchley
London
N2 9PT
Tel +44 (0)20 8365 3869
Fax +44 (0)20 8444 0339
Email seal@saffirepress.co.uk
Membership and Administration

SEAL
37 Park Hall Road
London N2 9PT
+44 (0)20 8365 3869
seal@seal.org.uk

Web www.SEAL.org.uk

ENGLISH TEACHING *professional*
Tech West House
10 Warple Way
London
W3 0UE
Tel +44 (0)20 8762 9600
Fax +44 (0)20 8749 6916
Email etp@etprofessional.com
Web www.etprofessional.com

EDU-KINESIOLOGY FOUNDATION
(EKF)
12 Golders Rise
Hendon
London
NW4 2HR
Tel +44 (0)20 8202 3141
Fax +44 (0)20 8202 3890
Email ekukf@mccarrol.dircon.co.uk

Index